COVENTRY LIBRARIES

Please return this book on or before
the last date stamped below.

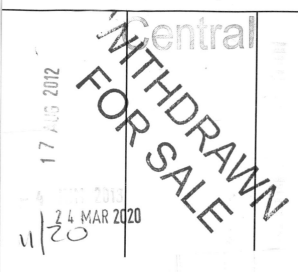

Central

WITHDRAWN
FOR SALE

17 AUG 2012

- 4 JUN 2013

2 4 MAR 2020

11/20

D1080743

To renew this book take it to any of
the City Libraries before
the date due for return

Coventry City Council

EMMA
WATSON
THE BIOGRAPHY

DAVID NOLAN

JOHN BLAKE

Published by John Blake Publishing Ltd,
3 Bramber Court, 2 Bramber Road,
London W14 9PB, England

www.johnblakepublishing.co.uk

www.facebook.com/Johnblakepub   facebook

twitter.com/johnblakepub   twitter

First published in paperback in 2011

ISBN: 9781843583622

British Library Cataloguing-in-Publication Data:

A catalogue record for this book is available from the British Library.

Design by www.envydesign.co.uk

Printed in Great Britain by CPI Bookmarque Ltd, Croydon CR0 4TD

1 3 5 7 9 10 8 6 4 2

Papers used by John Blake Publishing are natural,
recyclable products made from wood grown in sustainable forests.
The manufacturing processes conform to the environmental
regulations of the country of origin.

For Bonnie, who would like it to be known
that this book was her idea. Really, *really* like
it to be known . . .

CONTENTS

INTRODUCTION

Since her parents had split up, the little girl loved nothing more than spending the weekend with her dad – and nothing rounded off two days in London quite like tucking into his speciality dish: Sunday roast with all the trimmings.

Not that this was a rare occurrence. The split had been remarkably civilised – Mum and Dad were both lawyers, after all – and every other weekend the little girl and her brother would travel from Oxford to stay with their father in the capital. Afternoons in the park, shopping trips, stories at bedtime – all the expected things would happen. Not too much television, mind you. Dad wasn't really that keen on TV and movies.

But that weekend was a little different. For someone of her age, the little girl had a lot on her mind. She sat at the table – all blonde hair and button nose – with a slightly worried expression on her face. She'd auditioned for a part – a part in a film no less – and she really wanted it. *Really* wanted it. 'I just felt like that part belonged to me,' the girl would later remember. 'I know that sounds crazy, but from that first audition I always *knew*.'

The film was based on a book she knew well – a wizarding story that her dad had read to her many times over, during long car journeys or at bedtime. As Dad carved the roast chicken, he caught his daughter's eye – they'd both been looking at the same thing: the wishbone. If you pull a wishbone and think of the thing you hope for most, the wish will come true. Everyone knows that.

More than a decade later, the little girl would be a young woman – rich and famous to a degree that most people would find difficult to imagine. But she never forgot that day and never forgot what her dad did next. 'He gave me the wishbone,' Emma Watson would later say, reliving the moment just before her life changed beyond all recognition. 'I obviously made the wish that I would get this role. I still have that wishbone in my jewellery box.'

ONE

A QUEEN, A FAIRY, A PRINCESS OR A MATTRESS

I t's the kind of coincidence that a writer of fiction would probably steer clear of: it's a bit too neat, too easy, too convenient to be truly credible. But the fact is that Emma Watson came into the world at almost the same time as the fictional little girl with whom she will forever be associated.

Emma Charlotte Duerre Watson was born on 15 April 1990 in Paris, France. Hermione Jean Granger appeared fully formed in the imagination of Joanne – later J. K. – Rowling a few weeks later on a train from Manchester to London. The circumstances, though, were very different.

Emma's parents met at Oxford University, Britain's oldest university and still, much to Cambridge's annoyance, ranked the best in terms of results. 'When my dad talks about his time there,' Emma later explained to *Interview* magazine, 'he says it was the most incredible experience.'

Her parents were, from the start, a formidable pairing.

1

'My parents are both pretty high achievers,' Emma would later state. 'It's quite hard to win their approval.' Her French-born mum, Jacqueline Luesby, is a trained lawyer, fashionable – often seen in Chanel – and sporty with a particular talent for hockey. Jacqueline's love for the game would be passed to her daughter. 'It's my favourite sport,' Emma said. 'My mum played for East of England, which is why I think I love it so much, and it helps to take my mind off everything.'

Dad Chris Watson, a fluent French speaker, had also trained as a lawyer and would go on to forge a considerable reputation in the field of business competition law. A keen music fan with a fondness for blues artists such as B. B. King and Eric Clapton, Chris Watson is a man with a love of fine wine and even finer clothes. 'Dad loved his Hermès ties,' Emma later told *Tatler*.

Chris and Jacqueline were also both keen table-tennis players – and their approach to the game reflected their take on life: they played to win. 'My parents played and they're both really competitive,' she explained to *Mizz* magazine. 'They never used to let me win, but I got quite good at it.' In later life, Emma would stage table-tennis matches on the film sets where she spent much of her young life. 'Dan [Radcliffe] and Rupert [Grint] were quite taken aback that I could beat them. I think Rupert took it the worst.'

The young Emma seemed to react to her glamorous parents in very different ways. 'My mum could be fearsome,' Emma later told *Vogue*. 'She doled out the discipline.' Dad Chris, though, was – and still is – 'up there on a pedestal' in Emma's eyes. Journalists who interviewed Emma in later life often commented how regularly her dad Chris came up in her conversation. What's more, it would always be in glowing terms.

The young power couple decamped to Paris in the late eighties. 'I have a great nostalgia for it,' Emma would later recall about the city of her birth. 'I really love it. It feels a bit like home.' In later life, she would use the trips to Paris made available to her courtesy of French fashion houses to visit her beloved grandmother. Chris Watson's love of all things French and his taste in wine would lead him to be a vineyard owner and, in later years, Emma's summers would be spent visiting the land he owned.

Two years later, brother Alexander was born. It was around this time that the seed of a dream – one so common to little girls of that age – was first sown in Emma's mind. She would share the dream – in her own slightly skewed way – with her family. 'One of my grandma's most favourite "sitting round the fire at Christmas" stories is that when I was three she said to me, "What do you want to be when you grow up?"' Emma later explained to US talk-show host Jay Leno. 'I said I want to be a queen, a fairy, a princess . . . or a mattress. I meant actress, obviously.'

Not that being an actress – or indeed a mattress – was a particularly realistic option and the voicing of this early ambition must have struck her family as a charming if slightly unusual one. The picture Emma would later paint of her family life would be an extremely happy, if slightly dry, one. Being from a sturdily intellectual family meant that talk of a life in the entertainment industry was not something that tended to crop up at the dinner table. Theatre was part of family life, but movies just didn't appear on the Watsons' radar. 'I came from a background of lawyers and academics,' she later told the *Daily Express*. 'We just didn't watch films in our household.'

Cartoons seem to have been an exception, though, and Emma liked to dress up as her favourite Disney characters, often going to the shops in a Snow White costume. The 1989 Disney fairytale *The Little Mermaid* was a particular favourite. The film told the story of Ariel, a mermaid princess who, despite her status underwater, yearns for another life totally different from the one she knows: dry land.

Emma would hold one memory from her childhood especially dear – of dad Chris dressing up as Ariel's father King Triton as a surprise for her fifth birthday party. Not that young Emma was a total angel. 'I was such a drama queen,' she would confess to the *Daily Telegraph*. 'I used to wail and moan and cry, and little things were blown up into being big things. I don't know how my parents stood it, really.'

But, behind the seemingly idyllic, bohemian exterior, the Watsons were falling apart as a couple. By the early summer of 1995, they decided to separate. Jacqueline Watson wanted to head home for the comfort of Oxford and returned to Britain with five-year-old Emma and two-year-old Alex. Chris would also return to England, setting up home in the upmarket London enclave of Hampstead. The Watsons' lawyer instincts kicked in and arrangements for joint care of the children were agreed upon. Emma and

Alex would stay with their mother during the week and go to London every other weekend to see their dad. The Watsons seemed to have adopted a very British, heads-down, let's-get-on-with-things attitude to the split and to parenting in general. Despite Emma and Alex being so young, 'kids' stuff' was very much frowned upon. 'We would never be allowed to order off the kids' menu in restaurants,' Emma later revealed to journalist Lesley White of the *Sunday Times*. 'I wasn't babied. I was expected to step up when I was told to.'

In 1995, shortly after her return from Paris, Emma started at the prestigious Lynams pre-prep school in Oxford, where four- to eight-year-olds go to prepare for life at the main Dragon School, of which it is a part. It was founded in 1877 as the Lynams Preparatory School and many of its early staff were former Oxford University academics. The most prominent among them was a Mr George. When pupils picked up the nickname 'Dragons' – as in Mr George and his little dragons – it stuck, and the school was renamed soon afterwards.

The two parts of the school retain a rather raffish, informal air and pupils are encouraged to call teachers by their nicknames. Parents can expect to pay £20,000 for their children to board at the school and former pupils have the marvellously Potteresque name of Old Dragons. Among their number are tennis player Tim Henman, Ed O'Brien, guitarist with rock band Radiohead, and Hugh Laurie, the comic actor and star of international TV hit *House*.

By 1996, Emma had settled into a life split between her

parents – 'juggling' them as she put it – spending time in both Oxford and London. She would later remember going to London's Oxford Street in November of that year for the annual switch-on of the Christmas lights. That year, the lights were illuminated by girl power: the switch was flicked by the Spice Girls, riding high after the success of their debut single 'Wannabe'. Eight years later, the same ceremony would be performed by international film star Emma Watson.

Despite the split, the way in which Chris and Jacqueline conducted themselves in relation to their children – and their elder child's later fame – appears to be a model of how adults should behave when a relationship goes wrong. In public, they would continue to show a united front on all matters related to Emma, even going to film premieres together to show support for their daughter when fame later engulfed her. 'I rely on them hugely,' Emma confessed to the *Daily Mail*, 'and always speak to them first about everything.'

Emma would eventually become the big sister to a complex and elongated brood of step- and half-siblings on both sides of her two families. 'I have a quite complicated family life,' she would later explain to *Girl's Life*. 'My dad is remarried and he has three children [Toby and twin girls, Lucy and Nina]. My mum has a new partner, and he has two kids. Then I have a real brother called Alex, so I'm one of seven now. They keep me really down to earth. I mean, I can't get away with anything. They'll just be like, "Oh, here we go. She's going to completely over-dramatise and exaggerate everything," which I do have a tendency to do.'

Emma's dramatic powers would start to come to the fore

with a developing interest in poetry and acting. In later years, she would often make a point of highlighting her family's lack of interest in the world of film. 'I didn't come from a background of films,' she explained to the *Daily Mail*. 'I didn't even really ever watch films. The fact is, my parents weren't into that stuff, and neither was I.'

Despite this, several actresses did start to make their mark on the youngster: she would later cite Julia Roberts as being her 'favourite of all time'. Goldie Hawn and Sandra Bullock also appealed to Emma. Thoughts of acting – *could I do that?* – began to grow a little stronger, in some ways acting as a distraction to her complex home life. 'I'd been brought up in France, then moved to England, and I was adjusting a lot. And I think that any kind of acting is escapism. When you're performing, the whole of your body is consumed – you're so totally in the moment, you can't think of anything else.'

But if neither side of Emma's family could provide the artistic impetus she began to crave, then perhaps it could come from her school. Lynams put great store in providing chances for children to perform, and Emma's class was encouraged to learn a poem a week to help with their self-confidence and voice projection. There was even a school prize for the best poetry performance. Originally known as the Daisy Pratt Prize for Baby School Recitation, the award was named after a formidable member of staff who worked at the school for 30 years shortly after the First World War. Daisy Pratt was keen to encourage 'clear and lively recitation', and after her death in 1950 the tradition continued with a school poetry competition in her name.

Emma's performance side shone when she was just seven, when she won the Daisy Pratt prize with her rendition of 'The Sea' by children's writer James Reeves. The poem's text compares the sea to a hungry dog with 'shaggy jaws'. There's a lot of gnashing and rolling, tumbling and howling in the poem – it cries out to be acted out in big moves and grand gestures. It's not a poem to be performed by the shy and retiring – and Emma loved it. 'I loved finding out the real meaning of all the words, and how I could say them, and what I could do with my voice, and how I could get the audience to hang on my every word,' she recalled in an interview with *Marie Claire* magazine. 'I just got really into it.'

More performance opportunities came at the school – and at the Oxford branch of the children's theatre school Stagecoach – with an appearance in Oscar Wilde's *The Happy Prince*. The piece is an adaptation of Wilde's short story about the friendship between a statue and a little bird. Then there was Emma's first foray into the world of witches and wizardry. 'At my school we did a play every year, and I was very, very involved in quite a few of them,' she later told *Entertainment Weekly*. 'I had some main parts. You know, Arthur in the "Knights of the Round Table"? Yeah, I played the witch Morgan Le Fay, the evil sister of Arthur.'

Hard to believe now, but these 'lively recitations' and school plays were to be the extent of Emma's acting experience before her audition for the first Harry Potter film. It was just fun. 'When you're a young girl and you put on a tiara and a fancy dress,' she explained to journalist

Matthew Oshinsky, 'well, princesses, ballerinas, fairies, actresses, they all sort of come in the same bracket. It's all "let's pretend", let's just wear pretty things and be glamorous. It has no real meaning, or at least it didn't at the time for me.'

But, slowly, Emma's 'let's pretend' *did* begin to have meaning and she became, in her own words, 'obsessed' by being an actress. 'I dreamt of it,' she later confessed to the *Daily Telegraph*. 'I practised speeches in front of mirrors. Whenever there was a part at school, I went for it. I was probably a bit of a show-off in the sense that, any chance to get up and be seen, I did it.'

Meanwhile, the woman whose life was about to become permanently intertwined with Emma's was making some headway of her own. As seven-year-old Emma Watson was taking her first tentative steps at being a performer, an initial run of 500 hardback copies of a new book was being published. It was J. K. Rowling's first book and it was called *Harry Potter and the Philosopher's Stone*. Jo – she once said that the only time she was called Joanne was when she was in trouble – had ploughed a slightly chaotic route through life in the preceding years. Like Emma, she had lived in Paris, where she'd spent a year as part of her French and classics degree. She'd married a Portuguese TV journalist in 1992, had a daughter, Jessica, nine months later, and separated from her husband three months after giving birth.

After returning to the UK with her daughter and moving to Edinburgh to be closer to her sister, Jo lived on state handouts, writing in cafés to save money on heating. 'I had no intention, no desire, to remain on benefits,' Rowling told the *Daily Telegraph* in 1997. 'It's the most soul-destroying thing. I don't want to dramatise, but there were nights when, though Jessica ate, I didn't. The suggestion that you would deliberately make yourself entitled . . . you'd have to be a complete idiot. I was a graduate, I had skills, I knew that my prospects long term were good. It must be different for women who don't have that belief and end up in that poverty trap – it's the hopelessness of it, the loss of self-esteem. For me, at least, it was only six months. I was writing all the time, which really saved my sanity. As soon as Jessie was asleep, I'd reach for pen and paper.'

The grim reality of Rowling's day-to-day life – so very different from the privilege of Watson's – would soon become the stuff of magazine feature writers' dreams: 'Literary Triumph of Downtrodden Single Mum on Benefits'. Though true, it's a pigeonholing image that seems to annoy Rowling, particularly when it was subsequently suggested that the story was PR spin. In 2006, she explained her irritation to Channel 4's *Richard and Judy* show: 'Not to crack out the violins or anything, but if you've been through a few years where things have been very tough – and they were very tough – and it's dismissed in half a sentence, "starving in a garret", and occasionally I've thought, Well you try it, pal, you go there and see. It wasn't a publicity stunt, it was my life, and at that time I didn't know there was going to be this amazing resolution. I thought this would be life for twenty years.'

The original idea for the book had come to her in June 1990 (several weeks after Emma was born) as Jo Rowling was travelling from Manchester to London on a delayed train. It's become part of Potter folklore that the world of Harry Potter came to her in one overwhelming creative wave. 'I didn't know then that it was going to be a book for children – I just knew that I had this boy, Harry. During that journey I also discovered Ron, Nearly Headless Nick, Hagrid and Peeves. But with the idea of my life careering round my head, I didn't have a pen that worked! And I never went anywhere without my pen and notebook. So, rather than trying to write it, I had to think it. And I think that was a very good thing. I was besieged by a mass of detail and if it didn't survive that journey it probably wasn't worth remembering. So I got back to the flat that night and began to write it all down in a tiny cheap notebook.'

She began to weave a story about the orphan Harry Potter, who is transported from the grim suburban life he endures with his guardians when he discovers he is a wizard. Sent off to the Hogwarts School of Witchcraft and Wizardry, he makes friends with fellow young wizards Ron Weasley and Hermione Granger and with equal ease makes an enemy out of another pupil, Draco Malfoy.

Harry, Ron and Hermione uncover the magical stone of the title, which has the power of immortality. An evil wizard called Voldemort needs the stone to restore his powers. Voldemort killed Harry's parents – when the boy wizard discovers this, he vows revenge. Harry has to use all his cunning – and the help of his newfound friends – to get to the stone before the evil wizard does.

One of the characters was particularly close to Rowling's heart: Hermione Granger. In the first of the Potter books, Hermione is first spotted on the Hogwarts Express heading for the school of magic. She's described as having big teeth, big, brown, bushy hair and – most importantly – a very bossy voice. She would use this voice to rather annoying effect, criticising Ron's ability to cast spells.

Rowling has repeatedly described herself as being 'annoying' as a child. 'I'm quite open and I say that Hermione was at least partially based on me when I was younger,' she would reveal to NBC. 'I loosened up quite a bit as I got older, and so does she through the books, under the healthy influence of Harry and Ron. Hermione's a bit of an exaggeration. But I was deeply insecure, as is Hermione. She's covering up a lot of insecurities by trying to get good marks and so on. That's the place she feels most secure, in the classroom with her hand up.'

Rowling managed to get a literary agent, Christopher Little, to help her find a publisher – a dozen turned her down before Bloomsbury editor Barry Cunningham took an interest. 'Harry Potter came along because Jo had been turned down by everybody already,' Cunningham told the *Writer Unboxed* website. 'I believe she chose her agent, Christopher Little, because his name sounded nice, but he was really an adult author's agent. I really don't think he had any other children's book authors, but he knew my background and knew what I was looking for, so he sent me Harry Potter. I'm sure he had read it, but I'm not sure he knew what he had. I read it, and really the sky didn't part and the lightning didn't come down, but I just really liked it.'

Cunningham recalled his first impressions of Jo Rowling to biographer Sean Smith. 'I thought she was shy about herself but very confident and intense about the book and, most importantly, confident that children would like Harry,' he said. 'She just *so* understood about growing up.'

Bloomsbury gave Rowling a £1,500 advance for the manuscript and advised her to use the initials J. K. so boys would not be put off reading a book written by a female. Barry Cunningham later recalled the gentle warning he gave to Rowling just before the first book was published: 'You'll never make money out of children's books, Jo.'

Three days after it was published, the book was the subject of a bidding war among American publishing houses. It went to Scholastic Books for $100,000 – Jo Rowling was news and the Harry Potter phenomenon had truly begun.

Shortly after publication, a copy of the book came into the office of British-born film producer David Heyman, who had several cult movies under his belt, including the drug-fuelled comedy *The Stoned Age*. He'd just started work on a cannibal western called *Ravenous*. Rowling's book promptly found itself on his 'low-priority' shelf alongside other stories that would be unlikely to make it to the big screen. That's exactly where it would have stayed if it weren't for production secretary Nisha Parti, who took the book home, read it and advised Heyman to do the same. 'I read it and was captivated,' Heyman later told the *Guardian*, although he admitted he thought the title was 'rubbish'. 'The writing was so vivid and the characters so easy to relate to: Harry the outsider, Hermione the swot, Ron from a big family, the battle between good and evil. I went to a school like Hogwarts, but without the magic.'

Heyman began an 18-month-long courtship and eventually acquired the film rights. He didn't set the bar too high in terms of his expectations for the movie. 'I thought it would be a modest film,' he told the *Daily Telegraph* in 2000. 'My *Chitty Chitty Bang Bang*.' He would become the architect of the entire Potter series, bringing Warner Brothers into the deal.

By now, with two more books under her belt – *Harry Potter and the Chamber of Secrets* in 1998 and *Harry Potter and the Prisoner of Azkaban* due in December 1999 – Jo Rowling was a very different person from the Edinburgh single parent she had once been. She was a millionaire and more than capable of calling the shots to protect her creation. The first film would be the start of an epic cinematic journey, and Jo Rowling wanted to make sure the journey was under her guidance, despite the fact that only she knew the outcome. 'The biggest thing by far was that I was looking for an agreement that said they would follow my story even though the rest of the books weren't written,' she told US broadcaster NBC. 'What I didn't want to do was sell the rights to the characters and enable them to do sequels that I haven't written. That was my worst nightmare. So I was quite happy never to have Harry Potter films if I couldn't get that guarantee.'

The film's director needed to be involved from the early stages. Chris Columbus – who'd helmed hits like *Home*

Alone and *Mrs Doubtfire* – came across *Harry Potter and the Philosopher's Stone* (or, as it was renamed for the American market, *Harry Potter and the Sorcerer's Stone*) thanks to his young daughter, who tried to coerce him into reading it. 'I said, "No, I don't want to read it, it's a kids' book,"' he later told US talk-show host Charlie Rose. 'I don't have any interest in it. I finally picked up the book, read it and fell in love with it. I said, "I have to make this into a film." '

Unfortunately for Columbus, his old boss Steven Spielberg was in the frame to direct the first Potter film. As a screenwriter, Columbus had a hand in Spielberg hits such as *Gremlins* and *The Goonies*. 'If Spielberg's going to do, it's not even worth thinking about,' he said. 'It's not even a possibility.'

When Spielberg pulled out, Columbus got the job. He's since admitted that he had become 'artistically stale' churning out films in Hollywood and saw the chance of working with new, untried performers as a way to reinvigorate his work. Columbus threw himself into the audition process to find three young performers to play the lead parts in the film. 'I thought, I can turn this into some form of interactive filmmaking and be an active participant. By hiring these kids who aren't accomplished actors, I can get in there and act with them. Basically, it was almost like acting school. Turn these kids into actors. And that was the passion behind it.'

Emma Watson had, meanwhile, become a fully fledged 'Dragon', moving out of Lynams and up to the main prep school. While she was at the Dragon, a fellow pupil, future comedian Jack Whitehall, and another boy took some of Emma's possessions and sold them online after she became famous. 'We found some socks with her name tag in, so we whacked them on eBay,' he later claimed in Scotland's *Daily Record*. 'We thought, She's doing well for herself, let's make some money. I can't recall what we got for the socks. It wasn't over a fiver. She wasn't my friend and didn't want to be my friend at school.'

Outside of school, she had settled into the routine of her life split between London and Oxford. Although Emma would repeatedly state that her childhood was happy, it wasn't, to use her word, 'consistent'. 'Although I think divorce has a huge effect on children and I'd never make light of that,' she told *Women's Weekly*, 'I have a good relationship with both parents. It's very rare to see an amicable and harmonious divorce, and it makes a huge difference to children.'

Consistency would have to wait. It would come later in surprising ways: from stage hands, makeup artists, cameramen and actors. Routine and consistency would be provided by the very world that took her away from her family. But for now the nature of a routine spent between two households – in Emma Watson's case some 60 miles apart – always meant one thing: a lot of travelling. Books were the means to pass the time. And Emma liked a particular series of books to while away the time: the Harry Potter books by J. K. Rowling. Dad Chris would read them to Emma and Alex on long journeys and as their bedtime story. Emma in particular was a convert from the very first book. 'Everything about the book, everything about J. K. Rowling's world, is thought down to the very last detail,' she later explained to *The Times*. 'You can pull apart the spells and they're Latin and they actually mean what they are doing. And all the names are so interesting and so unique and different and everyone has their own history. And how she's come up with all of this is just so amazing. At the end of each book, it's almost like an Aesop's Fable. Every time, every year, there is a lesson that Harry learns.'

Emma Watson was halfway through reading *Prisoner of Azkaban* – she declared it her favourite – when the young Dragons, along with hundreds of other schoolchildren across the country, were offered an opportunity to audition for a role in the film version of *Philosopher's Stone*. It would be the first time Emma had tried for a part beyond the school. Despite this, she threw herself into the task. 'I *sooo* wanted to be Hermione,' she explained to *Vogue* more than ten years later. 'Even if I'd been ill. Even if I was dying, I would have found a way to go to school that day.'

The producers weren't looking for some random yet talented little girl: what they were searching for was very specific. Producer David Heyman wanted a youngster who embodied the essence of Hermione Granger. She had to be suitably forceful, but still have an essential likability. 'There was no open audition,' Emma would later explain to journalist Derek Blasberg. 'They went all over England to find these characters, and not just drama schools. They came to my school and asked if they could put forward a group of twenty children between the ages of nine and twelve. They took my photograph in the school gym, and then I got a call three weeks later. I loved the books; I was a massive fan. I just felt like that part belonged to me. I know that sounds crazy, but, from that first audition, I always knew. At the beginning, they were casting the other characters as well – but I always knew I was going out for Hermione. She came so naturally to me. Maybe so much of myself at the time was similar to her.'

When Emma's name was called out at school assembly so she could be told she had got through the first round, she thought she was in trouble for not handing in homework or being late for class. What followed was a hefty series of interviews and auditions. 'Eleven auditions!' she told *Entertainment Weekly*. 'That's a lot. Rupert only had to go through three.'

Slowly, the producers whittled the girls down, finding out more about them as individuals. 'The vast majority of the auditions were them asking me questions about myself,' Emma later recalled in an interview with the *Daily Telegraph*. 'Then they started having me read, and I think the lines I was given were where I was talking to Harry about not going after [villain turned hero wizard] Sirius Black.'

There was another reason why the film's producers were interested in the young actors' own personalities. A huge part of the task ahead would involve being able to handle the intense scrutiny and pressure that instant fame would bring, as well as the gruelling international round of promotional activities and interviews that would lie ahead.

Emma would later recall meeting Rupert Grint at several

such auditions. Grint, from Hertfordshire, stood out from the crowd thanks to his shock of red hair. Like Emma's, his acting experience so far stretched only to school plays and theatre-school productions. He had entered the auditions after spotting an item about the casting on the BBC's *Newsround*. He came up with a novel approach to get the producers' attention. 'I'd sent in one application and had heard nothing back,' Grint later told the *Mail*. 'So I figured there was nothing to lose by being a little inventive.'

Rupert recorded a video to sell himself to the film's producers. 'My video was in three parts. I dressed up as a woman and did a little sketch in the character of my drama teacher, then I read some Ron Weasley dialogue.' The third part was a rap: 'Hello there, my name's Rupert Grint, I hope you like this and don't think I stink . . .'

Tom Felton – who would win the part of Draco Malfoy – also remembered seeing Emma during the audition process. 'The crazy thing about the audition was that at my very first audition – when they had thousands of kids in, day in day out – Emma Watson was standing next to me and we did it together. And I came back in two weeks and she had been cast!'

As the auditions progressed, young Emma was alarmed to see a well-known child actress – who'd already appeared in a movie – taking part in the auditions. She would later recall 'crumbling' at the sight of the girl; was there any point in carrying on? Here was someone who had already done an actual film, who knew how to 'do it'. Surely, she had no chance. To make things worse, the girl was 'bonding' with a boy in the running for the part of Harry during breaks in the process – Emma spotted the two children playing cards together. 'I was like, "Oh, my God, they're making friends already! I'm definitely not going to get it. I was so, so upset. I wanted it so badly.'

As other girls fell by the wayside, Emma's desire to be Hermione increased; in her words, the best way of getting the role was to 'rehearse and rehearse and rehearse'. Her obsession – her compulsion – with getting the role began to 'terrify' her parents, who worked hard to manage their daughter's expectations. Emma made videos of herself practising for the next round of auditions, watching them over and over again. 'I started working on the audition at nine in the morning and didn't stop until five in the evening,' she recalled in an interview with *Marie Claire* magazine. 'The tape was just me doing the same thing hundreds of times over, until I got it exactly right. I was just amazed at my stamina. The grown-ups said, "We had to stop you; you wanted to keep going." I've always been like that. I give 100 per cent. I can't do it any other way.'

Producer Heyman clearly hadn't taken to the card-playing, experienced actress: Emma – whom he would later describe as being 'astonishingly bright . . . radiant and relaxed' – was moving up the running order. But Heyman was still looking for his Harry, too. A night out to see the Irish play *Stones in his Pockets* in London would soon change that. The play is about the dramatic effect becoming involved in a film production has on a small community. 'One night, looking for a break,' he would later explain to the *Los Angeles Times*, 'I went to the theatre with screenwriter Steve Kloves [who went on to write all of the Potter films apart from *Order of the Phoenix*]. There sitting behind me was this boy with these big blue eyes. It was Dan Radcliffe. I remember my first impressions: he was curious and funny and so energetic. There was real generosity, too, and sweetness. But at the same time he was really voracious and with hunger for knowledge of whatever kind.'

In fact, Radcliffe's parents had already said no to the role on his behalf, believing the pressure of a big-budget potential franchise would be too much for him. They had both been actors, but by the late nineties his mother had become an acting agent and his father a literary agent. Daniel was already an old hand. He'd appeared in a BBC adaptation of *David Copperfield*, playing the title character as a young boy, and had missed the initial round of Potter auditions because he was filming the Pierce Brosnan movie *The Tailor of Panama*, which would be Radcliffe's big-screen debut.

After four months of auditions and interviews, Emma was called into the production office along with Rupert Grint, and the two youngsters were told that they had won the parts of Hermione Granger and Ron Weasley – or, in the businesslike language of the film industry, that they were being offered 'preferred-candidate contracts'.

'We were together,' Emma later said, describing the day she and Grint were summoned. 'We thought, Oh, my gosh, another audition! We were both together, and then we were told that we were chosen to be Ron and Hermione.'

It was the moment she had dreamed of for months. Emma would later recall that she asked Heyman to pinch her, to check that she wasn't actually dreaming. Dad Chris was there too – and immediately became her manager, steering her through the early years. Both Emma's parents would be involved in the contract negotiations that initially tied her to just the first two Potter films. The chances of any child performer being able to last the full run of the stories were considered slim to say the least.

Not surprisingly, it was hard for nine-year-old Emma to keep the news to herself. 'I rang my best friend literally minutes after I'd been told,' she later told the BBC children's programme *Newsround*. 'She answered and said, "So, have you got it?" I said yes and she went "aaaaargh!" I had to hold the phone out here so she wouldn't break my ear. She was almost more excited than me.'

There was to be another important telephone conversation for Emma – this one with J. K. Rowling herself, who rang the youngster to congratulate her on getting the role. The author had a lot invested in the casting of a part based so much on her own persona as a child. 'Emma Watson in particular was very, very like Hermione when I first spoke to her,' Rowling later told *BBC Online*. 'I knew she was perfect from that first phone call.'

With Emma and Rupert already in place, Daniel Radcliffe was the final young performer to be brought into the production. 'We saw so many enormously talented kids in the search for Harry,' said Chris Columbus in a statement released by Warner Bros. 'The process was intense and there were times when we felt we would never find an individual who embodied the complex spirit and depth of Harry Potter. Then Dan walked into the room and we all knew we had found Harry. We were equally elated upon meeting Emma and Rupert, who are perfect for the roles of Hermione and Ron. I couldn't be happier to begin work with such talented, inspiring young actors.'

Shortly after the trio was completed, photographs of the three started to appear online, along with enough personal information to potentially identify where they lived. Fearing they'd be swamped by the media, the Watsons acted swiftly. 'The announcement was on the Internet, everywhere, within five minutes,' Emma later recalled in an interview with *The Times*. 'My stepmother grabbed a bag of clothes for me and we all went to stay in the Landmark Hotel [in London]. The day after, I was doing a press conference for 50 journalists.'

Emma Watson's life had changed for ever.

TWO

A REALLY GOOD TRIO

The three tiny figures blinked at the rows of journalists pointing microphones and cameras in their direction. They'd never experienced anything like it. The reporters were all there to see *them*.

Daniel Radcliffe, sporting Harry Potter-style round glasses, sat in the middle behind a hefty wooden table. To his left was Rupert Grint, babbling on about living in a barn and cracking jokes about being paid in 'Muggle money' ('Muggle' being the term used in the Potter universe for people outside the magical world). On the other side sat Emma Watson – pretty, poised, dressed in purple and propped up with cushions so she could reach the microphones. The question posed was an obvious one: how did you feel when you found out you'd got the part of Hermione Granger? 'I don't have a word for it . . . I was pretty excited,' Emma replied in a clear, clipped voice.

The two boys sounded like regular, everyday lads – but this girl was clearly a cut above. 'I'm really looking forward to filming. So far it's sort of turned things upside down. I've never had anything like this happen to me before. It's going to be so amazing to see how things are done.'

When asked whether she was similar in any way to her character, the little girl was once again a model of politeness: 'I'm not top-of-the-form goody two shoes. I'd *like* to be top of the form.'

At her first public engagement, Emma Watson may have come out tops for poise and professionalism, but it was Daniel Radcliffe who melted the hardened hearts of the reporters at the press conference to unveil the new stars of the first Harry Potter film. 'I remember at the first press conference, he was so overwhelmed by the whole thing,' Emma would later recall to the *Daily Mail*. When asked by journalists what he did when he heard he'd got the part, Radcliffe replied, 'I cried, actually.'

Producer David Heyman rounded the press conference off by reading out a message from J. K. Rowling. It gave the credit for discovering the three youngsters squarely to the film's director: 'Having seen Dan Radcliffe's screen test, I don't think Chris Columbus could have found a better Harry. I'm also delighted to see that we're going to have a screen Ron and Hermione who can bicker as if they've been doing it all their lives. Chris's choice of three wonderful British actors in the leading roles shows how well he understands the spirit of these books. I wish Dan, Emma and Rupert the very best of luck and hope they have as much fun acting the first year at Hogwarts as I had writing it.'

The press conference was over. Emma and her young co-stars would have to get used to such things – thousands more interviews lay ahead over the coming decade.

With the journalists temporarily satisfied, there was the small matter of actually making a £100 million film to attend to. What's more, they had only six months to shoot it. The young stars headed for their new home from home, Leavesden Studios near Watford in Hertfordshire, where purpose-built sets were under construction.

Emma, Daniel and Rupert arrived at the studios together. 'Our first day was September 29, 2000,' Daniel Radcliffe would recall nearly ten years later in an interview with CNN. 'Me, Emma and Rupert had all travelled up that day in a minibus, and we sat on the back seat – which was undoubtedly my influence – pretending that we were DJs on a radio station.'

Emma said, 'I just remember the wide-eyed excitement and awe. I just came into Leavesden every day, just to be so excited about what I was going to see next. Every time I walked on to a new set or someone new did something new, it was all just so overwhelmingly exciting. It just went by like this [snaps fingers] doing that movie. I have some really fond, silly memories from that.'

The studios were on the site of a former aerodrome where Wellington bombers had been built and had already been used for films such as *Goldeneye*, *The Phantom Menace* and *The Beach*. It would become the *de facto* home of the Potter franchise.

A dizzying array of locations around Britain were also

used to bring the book to life. Gloucester Cathedral, Durham Cathedral, Lacock Abbey in Wiltshire and Northumberland's Alnwick Castle were all brought into play. 'It's not as glamorous as I thought it would be,' Emma admitted to *Entertainment Weekly* in one of her first on-set interviews. 'I mean, it's a lot more complicated, a lot longer days, more work.'

In order to make the film within the time frame set by the studio, Emma would be away from home for long stretches. But the little girl seemed to treat it with the kind of stoicism that many children approach being sent away to boarding school. There's even a sense that it provided something of a relief from the toing and froing that any child experiences when marriages break down. 'I didn't have much stability at home,' Emma told the *Sunday Times Magazine* nearly ten years after filming began. 'Making the films has been a constant in my life, very stabilising, even if people think the opposite. My mum was definitely a bit worried. I was going into the unknown. She could no longer give me advice or tell me what to expect or even that it was going to be OK. I was a long time away from her.'

To her mum's relief, there were some sections of filming that were close for Emma, as her home city of Oxford was used for location work. Oxford University's 15th-century Divinity School stood in as Hogwarts' hospital; its Bodleian Library was used as the wizarding school's library; and the Great Hall of Christ Church College acted as Hogwarts' grand dining room.

The scale of the buildings – and of the whole production – took Emma's breath away. 'I like the Great Hall – I thought that was really great,' Emma later told Jonathan Ross for his *Film 2001* programme. 'All the extras, all the tables, all the floating candles – I thought that was fantastic. There were so many people to rely on. Can you imagine relying on just Rupert and Dan to make sure they didn't stutter their lines up or go to the wrong place or get in front of the camera? Imagine relying on 600 children to get it right? Really hard work.'

Along with the hard work – four hours on-camera time per day – there were also on-set school lessons to attend. Emma took to this a little more readily than Radcliffe and Grint. 'When we were on set,' she told the BBC, 'we had a tutor to keep up with our school work – three hours minimum, five hours maximum, so we kept up and everything. I really enjoy school.'

·As well as filming and school, there was even time for some fun. The two young boys would tease Emma constantly about how posh she was. The young girl would take her revenge the best she could. Borrowing a hairstylist's label printer, she set to work to get back at the boys. 'I printed out about 20 of these stickers,' she later told US chat-show host Rosie O'Donnell. 'Pull my hair, kick me, punch me . . . and stuck them on people's backs. They didn't notice for about 20 minutes which was really funny.'

In turn, Radcliffe launched an attempted counterstrike against Emma, courtesy of a remote-controlled whoopee cushion. 'He tried it on me, but it didn't quite work,' she said. 'Then he tried it on someone else who was going to sit down on a massive sofa. When it went off, Chris Columbus, the director, said, "Cut! What is that thing?" And everyone burst into laughter.'

Despite – or maybe because of – the teasing and pranks, Emma was starting to like her young co-stars. 'They're very well mannered,' she observed coolly. 'As far as boys go.'

The cast and crew used golf buggies to get around the vast maze of sets. Emma had a customised bike to get from one place to another on time. Robbie Coltrane, playing kindly school groundsman Hagrid, took great delight in watching Emma, Rupert and Daniel use the film sets as their own personal playground. 'They'd throw things at each other and play their Game Boys,' Coltrane told *Entertainment Weekly*. 'They liked to get the makeup people to give them gashes. Daniel got one to give him a black eye, and he came in the morning and the other ones said, "Oh my God! What happened?" Columbus was wonderfully patient. He should be sainted. It's extraordinary how he gets performances out of them.'

But, when she wasn't having fun and getting her own back on the boys, Emma Watson – just as she had been taught from a very young age – wanted to 'step up', to absolutely do the best that she could during filming. Unfortunately, her drive to please ended up actually slowing down production. 'I wanted everything to be so perfect,' she later told *Flare* magazine. 'I would work so hard to memorise my lines and the scene. We would have to stop shooting because I was mouthing Rupert's and Dan's lines at the same time. That's something I had to get over.'

Columbus – who had vast experience in directing children, especially after his hit movie *Home Alone* – had his work cut out for him in dealing with such young performers. 'He had to guide us through it because we didn't know what we were doing,' Daniel Radcliffe later admitted on American TV show *Inside the Actors Studio*. 'They wanted to encourage us that is was make-believe, that all we were doing was what we'd done all our lives as kids . . . just pretend and make-believe and play.'

The young stars worked in short bursts and the style of filmmaking and the way scenes were shot was a reflection of the young stars' attention spans. Shots were short purely by necessity. 'Rupert had a tendency to laugh a lot during the first two films,' Columbus later told the BBC. 'So getting one line on the first film was a little difficult; second film, maybe two or three lines. The first film had a style where you could shoot the kid for one line and then you would have to cut away.'

Another technique that Columbus used was to treat scenes with the youngsters like a silent movie, so that he could talk them through the action, telling them exactly what he wanted. 'What I found so very helpful and considerate was that Chris Columbus just turned the sound off on the set, and we dubbed our lines in later,' Emma told *Paste* magazine. 'That way, he could give us direct instructions on what to do, and where the special effects were to come in. Now that added a lot to his schedule, but it was so generous of him. Consequently, he got relaxed performances.'

But Daniel was a bit of an old hand compared with

Emma and Rupert, something that the young actress became increasingly aware of as time went on. 'I don't come, like Dan, from a very actorly family, so I was Bambi in the headlights – I never had anyone to guide me,' Emma later explained to *The Times*. 'I hadn't been to [acting schools] LAMDA or RADA, and I had a chip on my shoulder about it.'

Emma's parents were keen to make sure that their daughter did not get carried away with her new life. 'When I heard I'd got the part of Hermione, my mother said to me it was very important to keep the friends I'd made already,' she told the *Daily Telegraph*. 'She told me that in the future it would be important to know people liked me for myself and not because of my career. I try to keep my social life up as much as I can. And my mum and dad made a really big effort for me to see my friends a lot. I even brought some of them up to the set, which was really good fun.'

There was also an on-set visit from the woman who had conjured the whole of Harry Potter's world into existence, J. K. Rowling. 'One of the most disturbing feelings, and yet wonderful as well, was the first time I visited the film set,' Rowling later told ITV. 'I walked into the Great Hall, and I'd drawn the director, Chris Columbus, sort of a rough diagram of how I saw the Great Hall. The production design manager had just done the most astonishingly good job, and that felt like walking into my own head. I just walked into this place that I had imagined for so long and there it was and it really looked exactly as I imagined it, and it was astonishing.'

Rowling's rare visits to the set would have a profound

effect on Emma, bringing out a little bit of that Hermione insecurity. 'I just really want her to *like* me,' she said in an interview with the *Los Angeles Times*. 'I'm always really keen to tell her how I feel and maybe it's a bit much. She is so down to earth and funny and witty. I definitely see Hermione in her. She's genuine and brilliant.'

In turn, Rowling would also sometimes find the set visits a little disquieting. 'They showed me the chamber where [Hogwarts teacher] Quirrell faces Harry at the end of *Philosopher's Stone*,' she said. 'There was a spooky, spooky moment when I was stood in front of the Mirror of Erised, seeing myself, of course, exactly as I am.' In the book the mirror shows the 'deepest and most desperate desire of our hearts' – Erised is Desire spelled backwards. 'So I was seeing myself as a successful, published author,' Rowling recalled. 'So that was a very, almost embarrassingly symbolic, moment.'

A bad winter meant constant delays to filming, pushing the end of schedule past March as planned and into July. Producer David Heyman had to extend the applications for Emma, Daniel and Rupert to miss more school and be tutored on set. By July, filming was finally done – the occasion was marked in the way any right-minded young girl would mark it. 'I went on a clothes-shopping spree around London,' Emma later told the BBC. 'That was my treat.'

It would be a rush to get the film into cinemas by November – and to an extent it shows. 'Could have been better' was Chris Columbus's verdict when asked how he felt about the finished product on America's PBS television network. 'The visual effects . . . we didn't have enough time. We had a wonderful team but we didn't have enough time to do the effects.'

Despite Columbus's misgivings, *Harry Potter and the Philosopher's Stone* is still a perfectly respectable start to the franchise. From its opening shot of an owl on a sign showing Privet Drive – the home of the dreadful Dursley family, the 'worst sort of Muggle imaginable' – to Harry's moving farewell to Hagrid on the platform of Hogwarts' train station, this is a totally solid family film

Philosopher's Stone has a lot of unglamorous leg work to do: it has the job of introducing the characters and setting the scene for the next ten years' worth of films, even though no one knew for sure that the series would run that far. That job is done efficiently and there are enough set-piece moments to stay with the viewer. Not to mention a parade of British acting talent, all here to prop up any misgivings the viewer may have about the young performers: Maggie Smith, John Hurt, John Cleese, Alan Rickman and, in particular, Richard Harris, whom Emma would later describe as the 'perfect' Albus Dumbledore, the headmaster of Hogwarts.

Harris had enjoyed – some might say encouraged – a public persona built around his hellraising exploits since his breakthrough film *This Sporting Life* in 1963. An international star in the 1970s, he had gone into semi-retirement in the 1980s before making a return in 1992 in Clint Eastwood's *Unforgiven*. Since then, up to his death in 2002, his career had enjoyed something of an Indian summer, as he picked and chose roles that took his fancy.

Initially, the idea of playing Dumbledore wasn't one of them. 'I didn't want to do the pictures,' Harris would later explain to journalist Prairie Miller. 'I never read the books, and I never will read the books. It's not my kind of reading. But the script was super. So I said OK, I'll do it.'

A key factor in Harris's decision was his 11-year-old granddaughter: 'She read in the papers that all the actors in the world were queuing up to do it, but that Richard Harris won't do it. Typical Harris, they said. Anyway, she rang me up and told me that, if I didn't go and play Dumbledore in the movie, she'd never speak to me again. And, since it meant an awful lot to her, I said OK, I'll do it.'

It's believed that Harris signed up to all of the planned films and took on the role for free, in exchange for a percentage of the profits – a 'Potter Pension', as it became known. But he seemed strangely pessimistic about the chances of seeing the job through: 'I'll keep doing it as long as I enjoy it, my health holds out and they still want me, but the chances of all three of those factors remaining constant are pretty slim.'

Dame Maggie Smith took a similarly pragmatic approach to accepting the role of shape-shifting Professor Minerva McGonagall. 'I look on the part as a sort of pension,' she later told the London *Evening Standard*. She had already performed with one of the film's young stars. 'Dan I'd worked with before: we did *David Copperfield* on television. He was so enchanting. I was so thrilled when he got the part.'

As Harry, Daniel Radcliffe looks as if he's stepped

straight from the front cover of J. K. Rowling's first edition, but his acting hardly leaps from the screen. He *reacts* more than he acts, but he's at his best when sharing the screen with Robbie Coltrane's Hagrid. Rupert Grint's performing style can at best be described as 'broad'.

One of the best aspects of the film, though, is that we get to meet Hermione Granger for the first time. As Hermione, Emma Watson is charming and only gently annoying – not as teeth-grating as the Granger sketched out in J. K. Rowling's book and certainly not as 'mental' and 'scary' as Ron Weasley describes her. One of the most persistent questions Emma would be asked about her onscreen counterpart for the next decade was: are you and Hermione alike? 'We're both very stubborn, determined, loyal, academic feminists,' she later told the *Daily Telegraph*. Good answer. Spoken like a true Watson.

It's on board the Hogwarts Express that we get our first ever glimpse of Emma Watson on screen. She appears at the carriage door of the compartment where Harry and Ron are demolishing a mountain of sweets. Daniel Radcliffe later pinpointed that moment as the key starting point of the three young performers' relationship. 'We bonded just like our characters,' he said. 'We all really like each other. The train-compartment scenes were the most fun, because it was just me, Rupert and Emma, surrounded by sweets, just laughing and joking the whole time.'

In the scene – unlike the two boys – Hermione Granger is already in her school uniform. Emma speaks her lines with crystal-clear received pronunciation as she mends Harry's glasses by magic and puts Ron firmly in his place.

'Hermione always has some snooty lines for Ron,' she explained to the BBC's *Newsround*. 'He gets the worst of it, really.'

For her cinematic debut, Emma is on screen for barely 90 seconds, but it's she whom you remember from the encounter, rather than Grint or Radcliffe. 'Oh, my God, that scene feels like a lifetime ago,' Watson would recall in a 2010 interview with the *New Zealand Herald*. 'At the very beginning, when everything was new, I was just full of wonder and amazement because it was such an exciting time in my life. But now I feel weirdly disconnected from that – it feels like another person, because it was so long ago. It's so hard to even remember back to then.'

As Hermione, Emma wears her hair much darker and bushier than her own – it had extensions and had been 'boofed up', in her words, to achieve that unruly Granger look. An early attempt during filming to replicate Hermione's rather buck-toothed appearance with the aid of false teeth was abandoned, as Emma found it difficult to speak in them. Despite this, a little light dentistry was required during production. 'I lost a front tooth on the first film,' she remembered during an interview with the *Sunday Times*. 'They had to put a fake one in my mouth every day to hide the gap.'

Whether she is zapping fellow pupil Neville Longbottom, or saving Harry and Ron from the clutches of snakelike, writhing tree roots, Emma does a sterling job of bringing Hermione Granger to life. 'Hermione's got some really good lines,' she told *Entertainment Weekly* in 2001, clearly relishing the part she'd fought so hard to win. 'One of them is, "I'm going to bed, before either of you come up with another clever idea to get us killed – or, worse, expelled!" I like her because she's really bossy and nerdy and all that kind of stuff. It makes her funny even though she doesn't realise it. She's a total bookworm and will do anything to get top marks. I mean, I enjoy school, but I'm not obsessed with school.'

One of the book's key characters is Hogwarts itself. We get our first look at the towers and turrets of the wizarding school as the pupils approach it by boat at night. 'I think the best thing which I was looking forward to seeing from the book was just the outlook from the whole of the school,' Emma explained to the children's channel CBBC. 'Because it describes in the book coming over in a boat across the river to Hogwarts and just the first view . . . that took us ages. We had to keep going aahh, wow, oooh – a bit like watching fireworks going off.'

Few people would argue with the sumptuous nature of the sets: production designer Stuart Craig – an Oscar winner for films such as *Gandhi* and *The English Patient* – would be a mainstay of the entire Potter series.

Emma's most complex scene was her encounter with a giant-sized troll in a Hogwarts toilet. To film the complex and destructive sequence, she had to 'eat dust for a week'. She had to dodge the crushing blows of the troll's club as porcelain and wood crashed all around her. 'I had to do lots and lots and lots and lots of stunts, which I think is one of the reasons I enjoyed it, but one of the reasons it was so hard as well. They had six cubicles and they had to put a safety mat underneath it. I had to climb on to six cubicles and I kept banging my head. I was darting under sinks to make sure the troll didn't hit me. I had to do loads of running through legs and scrambling around the place and the really annoying thing was that they haven't used all of the stunts which I did, which was really annoying – not good enough!'

On 4 November 2001, London's Leicester Square was turned into a Potteresque wonderland to mark the world premiere of the film. Five thousand children dressed in homemade hats and wizardly robes turned out to see the stars arrive at the Odeon cinema. Security was tight – it was barely eight weeks since the 9/11 terrorist attacks on New York's Twin Towers and there had even been concern that the premiere might be cancelled. 'This is a very positive film about friendship, loyalty and bravery and good winning over evil,' director Chris Columbus pointedly told reporters as he arrived. 'I hope it will provide a lift to anyone that watches it, especially in these times.'

As ever with movie premieres, an array of *celebrities du jour* were on hand to attend the first showing: Sting, Ben Stiller and Cher were there along with celebrity kids such as Brooklyn Beckham, though it's not clear how much of the film the two-year-old actually understood.

J. K. Rowling made a rare and rather brief appearance and took the opportunity to step out in public for the first time with her new boyfriend, Edinburgh GP and anaesthetist Dr Neil Murray. The press took great delight in highlighting Murray's Potteresque appearance with his dark hair and glasses. He and Rowling would marry within the following eight weeks. Before going inside the cinema, Rowling made it clear that the premiere taking place in London was her doing. 'I wanted a British cast and a British setting, because it is a British story,' Rowling told the army of reporters camped outside the cinema. 'And we have all that. I wanted the movie to have its world premiere right here, in Britain. And here we are. I still can't believe all this has happened. For a person like me, this is not a run-of-the-mill kind of night.'

Dressed in purple, Emma brought little brother Alex along to the London premiere, even letting him muscle in on some of the red-carpet interviews. She also took the opportunity to yell a hello to her grandparents via the massed ranks of cameras. Emma admitted to reporters that she was feeling 'a bit shaky' about the premiere. 'I'm so nervous I feel like I'm going to be sick,' she said.

Daniel Radcliffe sounded fairly tense, too: 'I'm almost numb with nerves and that's never happened before. My face and my stomach are buzzing. I woke up at 3am, 4am and 6am, and, although I'm very nervous, I'm also extremely excited and happy today.'

After the premiere, the question was: would the critics be as excited and happy about the film? It has to be said that reviewers weren't overwhelmingly in favour of it. The main failing they highlighted seemed to centre on the movie's slavish adherence to the source book. Emma was keen to knock this criticism back. 'I think it's really, really important to stay truthful to the books because they're fantastic books,' she told the Scholastic Books website.

'Chris [Columbus] is working really close with J. K. Rowling, and I think that's what makes the films so great – the fact that we work with the author, who has all of the images and inspirations in her head.'

The other chief criticism was that the film was just too long for children to sit through. This concern, too, was batted back. 'Fans would have been crushed if we'd left too much out,' director Columbus told *Time* magazine. 'My mantra has been [that] kids are reading a 700-page book. They can sit through a two-and-a-half-hour movie.'

The *Guardian* was typical of those in favour of the film: 'This richly accomplished entertainment spectacular, the quickest, zappiest two and a half hours you'll spend in the cinema. Emma Watson is the magnificent Hermione: imperious, impetuous but heart-breakingly loyal in the tradition of the subordinate Enid Blyton girl.'

The normally rather highbrow *Time Out* agreed, breaking out a considerable amount of exclamation marks to make its point: 'What a feast for children! Long, and engrossing. Kids will love it! Wizard!'

But not all reviewers were quite so enthusiastic. 'A lack of imagination pervades the movie because it so slavishly follows the book,' said the *New York Times*. 'The film-makers, the producers and the studio seem panicked by anything that might feel like a departure from the book – which already feels film-ready – so *Harry Potter and the Sorcerer's Stone* never takes on a life of its own.'

But even reviewers who didn't care for the movie still found space to praise Emma's performance. 'Ms Watson has the sass and smarts to suggest she might cast a spell of her own on Harry in the coming years and, one supposes, sequels,' the paper said in the same November article.

'I got thrown in the deep end on the first one, but the Harry Potter films have been a pretty amazing acting school,' Emma told the *Daily Telegraph* when asked about that first role. 'When I got the part, the only thing I had apparently was some natural acting ability. I didn't know anything about making a film, and there was so much technically I had to learn and understand.'

Despite her lack of experience, it appeared that Emma Watson had indeed 'stepped up' to the role. 'When I got the part,' Emma later confessed to the *Sunday Times*, 'People were like, "Why you?" And I just remember seeing a L'Oréal advert, and coming out with an American accent, "Because I'm worth it." That was my answer then. My answer now is . . . I don't know. I just really *got* her.'

Emma's ability to 'get' Hermione would get only the shortest of breaks: filming on the second instalment of the Potter series was just weeks away. But she was playing her cards close to her chest as far as any further films was concerned. 'I'm starting the second one in December and I'm not sure about the rest yet,' she told Jonathan Ross. 'I'm taking it one film at a time.'

Already, with her every answer, Emma Watson was proving herself to be the model professional. At the end of her interview with Ross, she shook him by the hand and told the presenter, 'Really nice to meet you.' This was borne out even further when Emma and her two young co-stars were sent on a US charm offensive on the chat-show circuit.

Emma fitted every preconceived idea of what a well-brought-up English girl should look and sound like as she answered the same set of questions over and over again on a series of TV studio sofas. What magic power would you like? 'I would make myself invisible so I could sneak into concerts and be near rock stars,' she said. What was the best part of filming? 'Probably meeting all the new people. It was amazing to meet all the great co-stars we act with.' Do you have a crush on Daniel or Rupert? 'No.' She answered them all – as if she were being asked for the first time – with charm and good grace.

Not only was she professional, she was now also very, very famous, rapidly becoming the best-known 11-year-old in the world. 'The funny thing is I never realised that I was going to be famous,' she told reporters at the film's launch. 'It never really occurred to me. I was just auditioning for parts and I just loved the character so much. I felt that I knew how to play her and I could be her, and Chris Columbus gave me a lot of confidence. And the fame thing never really hit home, it never did. When you're doing a movie, you're kind of in a bubble and you don't really realise the impact it's having on the rest of the world. It comes in these surreal moments, like a premiere or a film coming out, and I realised that I am famous, but most of the time I forget.'

As the young stars made the most of the red-carpet limelight, production staff were already prepping scenes for them to film for Part Two of the series. Time was clearly of the essence: the three children were growing up fast, and it was even claimed that producers were rushing into Harry Potter II to beat the onset of puberty that was heading for Daniel Radcliffe. A spokesman for Warner Bros said, 'The filming of the second film is a natural progression. As for Daniel's voice breaking, we will cross that bridge when we come to it.'

Whatever the future held, one thing was certain: Emma Watson would be for ever bound in the public mind with her co-stars Daniel Radcliffe and Rupert Grint. They had embarked together on a journey like no other – a journey that only they would ever truly understand. 'We are really good friends,' Emma said. 'It would be really hard if we weren't good friends. We've made a really good trio.'

THREE

I AM NOT GOING TO HUG HIM

Emma Watson's parents – although divorced – still acted as one in terms of their daughter. They had made several key decisions relating to Emma and her newfound fame. One was that they decided not to tell her how much money she was now earning as work began on the second of the Harry Potter films. 'It's easier that way,' Emma reasoned. Another was how they would choose to continue living their own lives despite their daughter's job as a movie star. The parents of both Daniel Radcliffe and Rupert Grint had given up their jobs to concentrate full time on helping their children through the Potter experience. Tellingly, Emma's career-minded parents did not. 'Both my parents love their work, it's a big part of their identity,' she later told the *Sunday Times*. 'And, if Mum's whole life revolved around me, she wouldn't have been at home for my younger brother.'

Despite being confident her daughter could cope, it didn't stop Emma's mum from being concerned about her. But the consistency that Emma lacked shuttling between her parents was starting to come from elsewhere. As well as the regular crew and on-set tutors, Emma had a regular driver, Nigel, to take her to and from the set. 'He drove me to that first audition, and he's been driving me ever since,' Emma told *Interview* magazine. 'He's like my best friend – he knows everything about my life. If you have to sit in the car with someone for two hours a day, you had better like him! I get very jealous when he drives someone else.'

Emma also had two on-set female chaperones – like two wonderful older sisters, she said. The world of Harry Potter was becoming the most regular part of her young life. 'I got a lot of love and affection on set, but being the only girl sometimes was tough.'

Reuniting with Daniel and Rupert for *Harry Potter and the Chamber of Secrets* was easy – the tight schedule between the first and second films plus the promotional duties in Britain and the US meant they had barely been apart. The press became fascinated by the nature of the relationship among the three. One of the most constant questions Emma would have to face over the next decade was just *how well* she liked her co-stars. She became highly adept at batting the query away. 'We get along great, but I don't have a crush on them,' she told *Girl's Life*. 'I know them too well. I do have to keep them on their toes and show them who's boss.'

If Radcliffe and Grint were indeed under Emma's thumb, the two boys did manage, on occasion, to get their own back. During one scene on *Chamber of Secrets*, they arranged for an extra to give her a fright. The extra had been covered from top to toe in tattoos by the makeup department and was lying in wait to surprise Emma on the Knockturn Alley set. The boys told her to take a look at something interesting that was behind a curtain in a shop window. 'I went and pulled back this curtain and there was this man – at a brief glance I thought he was practically naked – covered in tattoos, just sat there in this chair. Dan and Rupert were just laughing and laughing and laughing at me. Very embarrassing.'

The three had become a unit, with the relationship being compared to that of brothers and sister. The toing and froing of her family life in the 'real' world became more complex as her parents' new families grew, and changed, making her the big sister to several siblings. 'My family has exploded in the last two to three years, so it's nice to be the baby when I'm working,' she told the *Daily Mail*. 'I'm the youngest [of the three Potter stars] and I'm a girl, so Dan and Rupert are really protective of me; they are like my brothers. If I'm feeling a bit anxious or I need to talk something over with someone, Dan's the one I'll go to. We had this great weekend once. We were stuck in the middle of nowhere in Scotland in this castle. We were both meant to be in bed and I sneaked into Dan's room and stayed up watching movies all night, drinking Coke and eating M&Ms from the minibar. Rupert's the guy I go to when I want to be relaxed and have a good laugh. His dressing room is like a child's wonderland with every kind of game, every kind of sweet, every kind of whatever you can imagine. I go to him if I want to snuggle up on the sofa and watch television.'

Having read the *Chamber of Secrets* book, Emma was aware that Hermione spends a fair chunk of it stiff as a board thanks to a petrifying spell. Not an ideal way to show off her acting skills, but she was aware of how the character had developed since the first outing. 'It was her first year at Hogwarts, she's settled down a bit, chilled out a bit,' she told *AOL Movies*. 'She's not as obsessed with all the school work. It's a good film for her. She's got some really good lines – Hermione doesn't stick to two syllables, it's got to be about six. She's the only girl so she gets to boss everybody about – girl power – she kicks ass!'

When it came to directing *Chamber of Secrets*, director Chris Columbus had learned his lesson from the first film, where he'd been unhappy with the quality of the special effects. This time, scenes where the actors had to interact with computer-generated images were shot first, giving the team nine months to get the effects right. 'We started shooting three days after *Sorcerer's* [*Philosopher's*] *Stone* opened,' Columbus told US interviewer Charlie Rose. 'There was a certain sense of relief. The film had done well at the box office. The kids and myself started to feel a sense of relief. The author trusted us, the studio trusted us. Then we started to make the film we really wanted to make. We started to improvise a little more, we started to have fun with the material.'

'The second time round, we had experience behind us and knew the cast and crew,' Emma told CBBC. 'It was really good fun and everyone was a lot more comfortable with that.'

But Emma and her two co-stars were developing as film performers – and growing up before our very eyes on cinema screens around the world. Because she was the only girl, Emma's self-consciousness was even more acute. She was greatly relieved that, for the new film, Hermione's ratty hairdo would be calmed down a little.

'It's a bit of a new context when you're doing it on screen,' she later said in an interview with the *Daily Telegraph*. 'I remember, especially with the earlier films, Dan and Rupert would grow like a couple of inches by the end of shooting because it was so long, or by the time the film was released, and that was kind of crazy. And I remember on the second one I was still losing teeth, so that was interesting. It was kind of a weird experience trying to like make the whole growing-up process run smoothly. We kind of had to do it without anyone realising. Everyone always asks this question: "Is it really hard growing up on screen?" And I'm just like "Well, I've never grown up any other way, so I don't know." It's just kind of the way it's always been and you deal with it, I guess. It's just the way it is.'

'These kids are actually becoming seasoned professionals,' Chris Columbus told Hollywood.com. 'It used to take ten or eleven takes to get to a certain point. Now it takes three or four. They're just very, very secure.'

The takes may have been getting easier for Columbus, but for Emma the nature of Hermione's character meant that sections of the script were almost designed to trip her up. 'There are so many scenes where I literally couldn't say my lines. Hermione gets such mouthfuls, it's like a tongue twister in each paragraph. She talks like a dictionary. She *is* a dictionary.'

Despite Columbus giving himself more time to create the special effects, the schedule would again be tight to get the film into cinemas by November. The crew returned to many of the locations used in the first film, but there would be new challenges too. Privet Drive was recreated at Leavesden Studios for the scene where Harry is rescued by the Weasleys with their borrowed Ford Anglia.

The rambling, slightly ramshackle world of Leavesden had become a third home to Emma – after her mum's in Oxford and her dad's in London – albeit a very unusual third home. 'You will be in the canteen and there will be all these witches and wizards and ghosts and ghouls queuing up,' she told the *Daily Mail*. 'I get a reality check whenever my family or friends come and a centaur goes galloping by. They'll be sitting there staring but I just don't see it because I've never known anything different.'

Cast and crew also ventured outside Leavesden: Black Park in Buckinghamshire was used as the Forbidden Forest and production was shifted to Ealing studios in west London for two weeks to film scenes in a large-scale water tank.

Richard Harris returned as Dumbledore. The veteran actor took great delight in working with his young co-stars, telling the BBC he was 'envious' of Emma, Dan and Rupert. 'Their heads are in a place that we have grown out of. There is a place that's committed to fantasy, and their heads are in the right place, and their souls are in the right place.'

For animal lover Emma – she had two cats, Bubbles and Domino, at her mother's house in Oxford – one of the delights of *Chamber of Secrets* was working with animals on set, including Hagrid's dog Fang. 'I really love animals and enjoy working with them. It can be quite hard. It's very hard to tell a dog, "Do it again, you weren't sitting in the right position." You have to be quite patient because Fang drools everywhere. It takes ages to get [it] off your robes, and Hedwig flies in the wrong direction. Most of the time they get it right, which is absolutely amazing! Their trainers must have the hardest job ever.'

There were new cast members joining the family, too: Liverpool-born Jason Isaacs devoured all four of the Potter books in one go before auditioning for the part of pure-blood wizard Lucius Malfoy, the father of Harry's Hogwarts arch enemy, Draco. Isaacs says he was made to feel more than welcome by the cast. 'It was like turning up to a very good party where all of the people are just slightly bored of each other and are thrilled when the doorbell rings,' Isaacs told the BBC. 'They were terribly welcoming.' Malfoy, with his mane of white hair, walking cane and condescending voice was, in Isaacs's words, 'completely supreme in his arrogance and his ruthlessness'.

A very different kind of arrogance was on display thanks to another new addition – preening celebrity wizard Gilderoy Lockhart, played by Kenneth Branagh. 'Lockhart is the new Defence Against the Dark Arts teacher,' Branagh told *Total Film*. 'An apparently fantastically successful wizard and writer whose books are now being used as textbooks at Hogwarts. He is a narcissus, a gadfly, very full of himself and faintly idiotic. But he can also be rather touching at times. He is certainly a strange peacock of a man. J. K. Rowling describes Lockhart in a much more impressionistic way than many of the other characters. She talks of his "flowing golden locks", which we've tried to match with an excessive hairdo. She also talks of his dandyish quality, which Chris Columbus was keen to exploit. Lockhart's character is a chance to splash some colour into the movie.'

J. K. Rowling had spent a great deal of time denying that many of her characters were based on people she knew. Not so with Lockhart: 'I have only once set out to depict somebody I have met,' Rowling later explained on her website. 'The result was Gilderoy Lockhart. I assure you that the person on whom Gilderoy was modelled was even more objectionable than his fictional counterpart. He used to tell whopping great fibs about his past life, all of them designed to demonstrate what a wonderful, brave and brilliant person he was. Perhaps he didn't really believe he was all that great and wanted to compensate, but I'm afraid I never dug that deep. You might think it was mean of me to depict him as Gilderoy, but you can rest assured he will never, ever guess. He's probably out there now telling everybody that he inspired the character of Albus Dumbledore. Or that he wrote the books and lets me take the credit out of kindness.'

In Emma's view, there was one person who definitely did not think Lockhart was objectionable: 'Hermione is seriously dreamy about Lockhart – he is the Brad Pitt of her day.' She seemed almost as enthusiastic about Kenneth Branagh. 'He is the nicest guy,' she told the Scholastic website. 'He is absolutely fantastic. He's really down to earth, really friendly, and he has a great sense of humour. I really liked working with him. He's a fantastic actor as well. There's such a presence about him.'

Columbus continued with his hands-on directing style with the young stars he began with on the first film. 'It feels like he's in there with you,' Emma told journalists at a press conference to promote the film. 'It's not like he's standing at the monitor and goes "cut". Before every take, Chris would say "go sprint". So I would literally have to run or do star jumps and stuff just to get excited because we could get really tired.'

Emma maintained her energy levels on set by eating her favoured chocolate bars – Crunchies. Daniel's chocolate of choice was Mars bars. Rupert Grint appears to have been not too fussy about what sweets or chocs he got his hands on. Perhaps because of this – plus the onset of their teenage years – the young stars began to appear a little less fresh-faced than on the first film. 'Thankfully, the boys were going through spots at the same time,' Emma told *The Times*. 'So we had a dermatologist doing the rounds. She gave me something that burnt the skin off my face. It was terrible. They couldn't hold filming; we just had to put more makeup on, which made it really sore. The head of makeup promised me she wouldn't let them put anything out there where my skin looked bad, and I had to trust her. But it took a lot out of me to put myself in front of cameras with my skin like that.'

They may have been growing as performers, but these were still young people on the brink of adolescence – that most sensitive and awkward of times. One moment on set would highlight the entire issue. 'I asked Emma to hug Dan,' said Columbus, 'and she said, "No way," and that was the day she was the most nervous being on the set. She was like, "I am not going to hug him, no I'm not." And I said, "You've been petrified, this is one of your best friends, if not your *best* friend, you have to hug him," I said, "but you *won't* hug Ron, because *that's* where the tension is.'

'At the time I was, like, "You've got to be kidding me,"' she told *Newsround*. 'You want me to run all the way down the Great Hall and throw my arms around Harry? I was, like, "No way – I'm not doing that." I was so embarrassed. The only way I'll do it is if you don't do it in slow motion and you don't put soppy music behind it.'

Try as he might, director Chris Columbus could only get Emma to give Daniel the briefest of embraces before she ran off to hide. Columbus said, 'So, basically, she had all her friends, all the actors, actresses, and she had to hug him in front of 350 actors. As a kid, she was terrified. So she hugged him, and I had to extend it through editing. She would hug him, and, at the next frame, gone.'

But filming wasn't all stressful for Emma. Robbie Coltrane could always be relied upon to keep her and the other cast members amused between takes. 'There were 300 extras in the same room for one whole week. Everyone is dying of boredom and they need to be laughing. Robbie Coltrane stood up on the tables and danced. They did the

Macarena and the cancan – and it worked! It was the highlight of the whole filming! I never laughed so much in my life!'

The final day of filming was an emotional one for Chris Columbus: he had decided to step down as director after two films. By a quirk of scheduling, the final shot was with Emma, Rupert and Daniel, the three young performers he had helped to choose. 'Nobody was sort of bawling and hugging; but it was the three kids and myself. We'd just done the library scene where Hermione finds the polyjuice potion. And I just realised that that was the last time the four of us would be working together in that capacity. So we just sort of walked off and talked a little bit. It was a sort of dry moment, and I kept undercutting it by saying, "We're going to see each other again . . . it's all going to be fine." It was extremely emotional. You have to hold back the tears, because there's a part of your life that's been going on for three years that now is no longer going to be there.'

Emma for one would miss Columbus: 'I don't think I'd have been able to do it if I didn't have a guy like him starting me off.'

On 25 October 2002, just as the publicity machine for *Chamber of Secrets* was gearing up, Richard Harris died. The veteran hellraiser had just turned 72. He had made 70 films over a 50-year career, but, to many younger cinemagoers, he would always be Albus Dumbledore. He'd been battling Hodgkin's disease throughout the filming of *Chamber of Secrets*, but there was no question of another actor taking over. Director Chris Columbus revealed shortly after Harris's death that the actor was adamant that he could carry on. 'He did threaten to kill me if I recast him; I can't even repeat what he said to me. We're all still in an incredible amount of shock. We knew Richard was sick but he was such a fighter that somehow deep down we all expected him to make it and get through it and be in the third Harry Potter film. So it's a complete shock because we've all worked so closely together. It's like losing a member of your family.'

'He is Dumbledore in many people's eyes,' producer David Heyman told *ITV News*. 'In truth he is irreplaceable. We will find a new Dumbledore but there will only be one Richard Harris.'

Harris himself, despite his outsized talent and personality, had been characteristically dismissive of his legacy. 'I'm not interested in reputation or immortality, or things like that,' he'd said shortly before he died. 'I don't care if I'm remembered. I don't care if I'm not remembered. I don't care why I'm remembered. I genuinely don't care.'

His Harry Potter colleagues did care, though: Emma had lost her 'perfect' Dumbledore – it would be 'very difficult', she said, to carry on without him.

'It was awful,' Daniel Radcliffe, speaking on behalf of his young co-stars, said. 'I have what I think is the kind of supreme, amazing honour of being able to say that I was in the last scene that he ever shot. I don't think Richard is the kind of guy who would've wanted us to mourn over him. He would've wanted us to be happy and just remember him for all the times he made us smile and just laugh.'

Harris's death cast a shadow over the film's premiere on 3 November in London. The subsequent press coverage also centred on how markedly Emma and her co-stars had grown up since the first film. 'Emma Watson looked every bit the sophisticated film star when she stepped out for the premiere of *Harry Potter and the Chamber of Secrets*,' said the *Daily Mail*. 'The gangly 11-year-old of last year had turned into a groomed, sleek young adult as she cast a spell on fans with her pink taffeta dress and strappy shoes at the star-studded event. Although she's grown taller by several inches, Emma is keen to carry on in future versions of J. K. Rowling's magical stories. "I just can't wait to start filming the new film," she said at the premiere. "I start in February or March."

'Emma is now a star thanks to the Harry Potter phenomenon but says she's remained true to herself and hasn't let her life change due to her success. "I get recognised, but you get used to that. There are worse things than being recognised," she says.'

Emma, wearing a purple coat to protect her from the chill autumn air, answered the usual questions from journalists about how excited she was and who she would turn herself into if she had some polyjuice ('Jennifer Aniston – so I could see if Brad Pitt was really that good-looking close up'). It was left to the grown-ups to answer the difficult questions. J. K. Rowling made an appearance – she was asked by reporters who would be the new Dumbledore. 'He's going to be very difficult to replace and I honestly don't know if they've even thought about who yet.'

There were other changes in the world of Harry Potter movies, other things for journalists to ask awkward questions about – such as why Chris Columbus was walking away. The first film was already on its way to being the second most successful film of all time after James Cameron's *Titanic*. To observers, it seemed crazy to walk away from such success. 'It's been two and a half years and I haven't had dinner with my own children during the week,' Columbus told reporters. 'I just wanted to see them. I mean I get to work at six in the morning and then I come home at ten at night, and I really just wanted to take them to school in the morning and be there for them because ironically they're the people who got me into the whole Harry Potter world, and now they're the people who are getting me out of it. They're not asking me to: I just made a decision. My son Brendan asked me, when I was almost finished shooting *Chamber of Secrets*, "Dad, are you going to do the third?" I said no, and he just gave me the strongest hug, like, "Thank you, thanks for coming home." So it's good. I've given a lot of time to these kids who are like my other family and now I need to give some to my other kids back home.'

The promotional machine shifted to America with premieres in New York on 13 November and Los Angeles the following day in preparation for the film opening on thousands of screens across the US. Emma hit the usual round of early shows and late shows to plug the film, along with Daniel and Rupert. She was a model of politeness as each of them was asked the same questions, and she feigned surprise as interviewers pulled out a Hermione action figure for Emma to pass judgement on. 'It was unbelievable seeing me as an action figure! In a few months, toddlers all around the country will be biting my head off!' she said.

On *The Tonight Show with Jay Leno*, she appeared alone, gamely playing along with the host's attempts at an English accent. She told Leno her story about wanting to be a 'queen, a fairy, a princess or a mattress' when she was three. 'At least I've achieved one,' she told Leno.

Accompanied again by little brother Alex – who was becoming quite expert in acting as chaperone to his big sister for movie premieres – Emma was then whisked away from the *Tonight Show* studio by limousine and then helicopter to make it in time for the Los Angeles premiere in Westwood Village. Emma had to get used to a new level of fame. 'I met Robin Williams when I was in New York,' she told US chat-show host Wayne Brady. 'He knew who I was! That's very cool. I met Halle Berry and I completely couldn't believe it when she said, "Oh my God, you're Emma Watson!" and I said, "Oh my God, you're Halle Berry!"'

It's not difficult to make a case for *Chamber of Secrets* being a better film than *Philosopher's Stone* on almost every level. From the Weasley brothers' daring rescue of Harry in a flying Ford Anglia and Dobby the house elf and his annoying overeagerness to please, to the spider attack in the Forbidden Forest and the superbly rendered Basilisk battle sequence at the climax, this is a family action film to savour. Columbus's decision to do the scenes where the performers interact with the computer-generated imagery

(CGI) early on in the process pays off: Dobby seems totally *real* when he's interacting with Harry in his bedroom at Privet Drive. Diagon Alley is brought to bustling life as Harry meets up again with Hermione – and Hermione once again fixes his glasses.

Emma is on top form as she stands up to Jason Isaacs's Lucius Malfoy. He sneers at her Muggle (non-magical) parents and her eyes brim with tears after Draco Malfoy calls her a 'filthy little mudblood' (the term used for someone who has magical powers but is of Muggle parents). Hermione is indeed petrified, as in the book – an almost-convincing dummy stands in for Emma – and she's off screen for 50 minutes, but the absence is made up for with that run through the Great Hall, ending in the hug that Chris Columbus found so hard to shoot.

But the acting honours surely go to Kenneth Branagh and his portrayal of Gilderoy Lockhart. He steals the show in a role that was at one stage earmarked for Hugh Grant. Whether he is unleashing a flock of Cornish pixies or turning Harry's arm to jelly after a Quidditch match goes badly wrong, Branagh manages to make Lockhart foolish but not totally dislikeable. 'I think there's a kind of instant understanding that this guy is an idiot,' Branagh told the *Examiner*. 'Only an idiot could have that much confidence and that much lack of awareness. He's in his own impregnable bubble of delicious narcissism. Several people mentioned that I was really sending myself up. There's an implicit assumption that I'm an egomaniac.'

Meanwhile, several actors were being mentioned in connection with taking over the role of Albus Dumbledore, among them Christopher Lee and Ian McKellen. Both actors would be associated in the public mind with the *Lord of the Rings* films, in many ways a rival franchise to the Potter series. It was even reported at the time that McKellen had at one stage accepted the role. 'People say to me, don't you wish you'd played Dumbledore?' McKellen later told the *Guardian*. 'I say no. I played Gandalf . . . The original. There was a question as to whether I might take over from Richard Harris, but, seeing as one of the last things he did publicly was say what a dreadful actor he thought I was, it would not have been appropriate for me to take over his part. It would have been unfair.'

There was even speculation that filmmakers were planning to use Harris's on-set stand-in to shoot the scenes, with Harris's face digitally added in post-production. The Internet gossipmongers would have to wait until the New Year to find out who would take over the role.

Reviewers tended to agree that the second instalment of the Potter franchise was a step in the right direction. 'The news from Hogwarts?' asked *Time Out*. 'After many adventures our brave, clearly older young knight Harry slays the dragon. The franchise is safe! Columbus's second alchemical movie ups the thrill quotient to satisfy the faithful. There's more action, and it's scarier.'

'Darker and more dramatic,' said *Variety*. 'This account of Harry's troubled second year at Hogwarts may be a bit overlong and unmodulated in pacing, but it possesses a confidence and intermittent flair that begins to give it a life of its own apart of the literary franchise, something the initial picture never achieved.'

The *Guardian* took the opportunity to flag up the changes apparent in the look of all the young stars, especially Emma. 'Daniel Radcliffe as Harry, Emma Watson as Hermione and Rupert Grint as Ron look distinctly older than they did the first time around,' said their reviewer Peter Bradshaw. 'Emma Watson continues on her well-made-up journey from baby to babe.'

Emma Watson, it would appear, was growing up.

FOUR

BEWARE: BABE INSIDE

Despite her obvious adaptability, Emma couldn't be educated on set permanently, so as she became a teenager she was enrolled at Oxford's Headington School. Parents of day pupils can expect to pay £3,500 a term for their children to attend Headington – for full boarders it's more than £7,000.

For Emma, school was the most normal aspect of her life, and, unlike many children of her age, she seemed to crave it. 'I'm trying to do exactly what I do before I even started the films,' she said. 'Between films I always go back to school, I see all my friends, I play sport and I go to normal teenage parties. All of my money is locked away in a bank. I have good friends and family who keep my feet on the ground and keep it real.'

The all-girls Headington School was established in 1915 and former Headingtonians include newsreader Julia

Somerville and TV dog trainer Barbara Woodhouse. The school motto is 'Fight the Good Fight of Faith'.

Each of the Potter kids would have his or her own fight to deal with in terms of schooldays. Emma admits she did face trouble from fellow pupils after her return to mainstream education, but seems to have dealt with it in a typically stoic, Watsonesque manner. 'Going back to school is all right,' she told *Newsround*. 'I go to a very big school and some people give me a bit of stick. They walk past and go, "*Wingardium Leviosa*" [one of the famous spells in the Potter films] for the billionth time that day, and I go aagh! But apart from that most people are really nice about it. My close friends just treat me normally. They ask questions about it because they're curious, but it's OK. It's funny mixing the two worlds, but I still do everything I used to do. I still play hockey and do all my sports.'

Daniel Radcliffe says he too was bullied, but the slightly built young actor used his growing confidence and sense of humour to avoid real trouble. 'Because I'd been on set with some really genuine witty people over the last few years,' he later explained to *Esquire* magazine, 'I could turn round to these idiots and try to tear them apart. I'm not saying I was Oscar Wilde at 14, but I had a line for anything they could throw at me.'

Typically, the easy-going Rupert Grint seems to have floated over any such problems, despite seeming like a natural target with his flaming red hair. 'My friends have been great – they treat me normally,' he told CBBC. In fact, Grint's only complaint seems to have been people at school being too nice to him. 'The teachers suck up, they really do. But other than that it's been fine.'

'I'd be lying if I said there wasn't any difficulty at school,' Emma told BBC Radio 4 in 2009. 'Hey, it can be tough but I stuck it out. I always loved school. I think it was different for the boys – Rupert and Dan never really liked it. I weirdly did. But even if I wasn't in a film, a bit of teasing and a bit of banter is just part of being at school. It's normal and you have to learn to get on with it.'

The person who seemed to have suffered the most was Draco Malfoy, Tom Felton. 'I would miss months of school and then return with bright-blond hair,' he told *Heat* in 2010. 'Needless to say, there was bullying. I wasn't beaten up daily, but there was name-calling and jealousy. You have to bear in mind that Harry Potter wasn't cool. I wasn't part of the *Terminator* franchise.'

In February 2003, the team started work on the third film in the series. *Harry Potter and the Prisoner of Azkaban* was the book Emma was reading when she got the part of Hermione. 'It's my absolute favourite of the books so far,' she said. 'Loving the third book so much is probably a bit selfish on my behalf because it is such a great part for Hermione. She really comes into her own in this novel. We get to see several different sides of Hermione.'

Daniel Radcliffe agreed. 'This is my favourite of the books,' he told *USA Today*. 'It's a weird one because it almost reinvents the character. He's more hostile. He's got a lot of teenage aggression, which all people at 13 do.'

The book had been published in July 1999 and J. K.

Rowling would describe it as the easiest book that she would write. The book marked the true globalisation of the Potter phenomenon. To promote it, Rowling went on a three-week coast-to-coast US promotional tour of signings, appearances and TV interviews. To dispel any final doubt about how far her creation had become ingrained in popular culture, in October 1999, Harry Potter made the cover of *Time* magazine. 'I have a very weird life at the moment,' Rowling told CBS News. 'Half my life is exactly as it was in the past. I spend my time doing housework, looking after my daughter and writing novels. You could describe it as dull. Then suddenly I come to America and it's wonderful. The number of people at the signings, the interviews and publicity is enough to make my head spin.'

With the new film, a very different kind of filmmaker was to be found in the director's chair: Mexican born Alfonso Cuarón had taken over from Chris Columbus, who would take on a producer's role for the new film. 'My biggest concern in hiring a director was deciding who would bond with the kids,' Columbus told the BBC. 'This was a very special relationship we had over the past four years and I wanted to make absolutely certain that they would be in good hands. When I met Alfonso and I saw how he was interacting with the kids, from the very first moment I knew that they were in great hands.'

Cuarón had come to prominence with the 2001 film *Y Tu Mamá También* (*And Your Mother Too*), a sexually charged road movie about two teenage boys and their encounter with a woman in her late twenties. 'Obviously the tone of the movies is completely different,' Cuarón told *USA Today* when asked to compare his best-known film with the new Potter. 'Y *Tu Mamá* was very realistic, with social observation. Here it's a magic world, a fantasy, a bigger canvas. But emotionally it's exactly the same thing. It's a journey of a character seeking his identity and accepting who he is. To step out of the shadow of his father, for instance, is one of the themes. And, as in the non-magical world, the characters' emotional lives have more intensity. The hormones are buzzing, and so is their anger about things. And rather than repressing those things, it's about letting it flow. It's not about encouraging it, but just letting it be . . . I didn't want those emotions very polished. Sometimes they got carried away. I would let them. I didn't want them to be neat. I wanted it a little raw.'

Y *Tu Mamá También* proved, if nothing else, that Cuarón knew how to direct teenagers. J. K. Rowling said, 'Alfonso was mentioned very early on, and I was really enthusiastic about the idea – and I loved Y *Tu Mamá También*. Alfonso just obviously understands teenage boys backwards.'

Indeed, producer David Heyman described Cuarón as a 'teenager at heart', making him the ideal choice to direct Emma and her two young co-stars. 'Well, teenagers recognise other teenagers,' the director told the BBC at the time. 'From the moment I read the material, it was something that I connected with. This is the story of a kid who is seeking his identity as a teenager and I felt it was something I knew how to make into a film.'

In taking over from Columbus, Cuarón had his work cut out for him. *Chamber of Secrets* had earned £10 million in its first weekend and another £55 million in its first three days across America. He clearly wanted to stamp his own authority on the new Potter movie but success was expected – on a large scale. Before filming started, he asked Emma, Daniel and Rupert to write an essay about their characters and about themselves to help him understand the essence of Hermione, Ron and Harry. The idea behind the essays, Emma told *Entertainment Weekly*, was 'not just to help us, but to help him see the character through our eyes. He gave us a lot of freedom with that as well.'

'The kids were very brave,' Cuarón told *USA Today*. 'They bared their souls. They were very eloquent. At some point, I wanted to publish them, then I thought no. I promised them it was just for the work of the film and it's their personal stuff.'

The end products of this exercise turned out to be highly reflective of the young actors, their personalities and the personalities of their characters. 'We ended up being freakishly like our characters,' said Radcliffe. Daniel wrote a nice, straightforward page. Rupert Grint forgot about it and never wrote a word. Typically, Emma – a high-achieving Watson – did nearly a dozen pages. Her co-stars would use this example of her eagerness to please as another way of teasing Emma – the number of pages she apparently wrote would increase with each retelling of the story. 'It gets more and more every time,' Emma exclaimed during a press interview when Radcliffe upped the number of pages she'd written to 20. 'It was 10, then 12, then 16, now 20? Come on! I have big handwriting, and I leave big spaces, OK?'

'These kids were starting to take themselves seriously as actors,' enthused director Cuarón. 'So they were willing to explore more emotional territories. I was so lucky that I had them so raw and so willing to go there.'

One of the places that Emma had to go was in bringing Hermione's budding interest in Ron to the screen. 'Hermione and Ron spend the whole film just arguing with each other,' Emma said. 'Ron is convinced Hermione's cat has eaten his pet rat. Their squabbles are a bit of a cover-up. They actually have a bit of a soft spot for each other. It's a classic love–hate relationship. You always tease the ones you fancy.'

Not everyone was quite so keen to see the first buds of romance between Hermione and Ron – Rupert Grint seemed faintly appalled by the prospect. 'I hope it doesn't happen,' he told *Entertainment Weekly*. 'I hope Ron gets killed off before they actually do something.'

Some of Ron and Hermione's onscreen interactions ended up on the cutting-room floor, including a moment where there was, as Watson put it, 'an awkward hug between them. Alfonso kept the scene in where they hold hands for a moment when they are frightened so I know audiences will see what is developing between them. I think Alfonso and [writer] Steve Kloves did a really good job on adapting *Prisoner of Azkaban*. Even though a lot was cut, they did a great job of making sure the really important things made it into the film.'

One such really important moment was a sequence that would sometimes prompt a round of applause during screenings: the 'foul, loathsome, evil little cockroach' Draco

Malfoy (Tom Felton) getting his comeuppance at the hands of Hermione courtesy of a swift punch to the face. Alfonso Cuarón recalled, 'Emma was looking forward to that moment, and I remember Tom telling Emma, "Oh, if you want to hit me, just hit me, just hit me."'

'I loved it – I loved every single second of it,' Emma told *Teen Hollywood*. 'Girl power – it was great! I would have done it for a whole week, but it was only a couple of takes. I went, "I want to do it again! I want to do it again!" It was great. It's a great moment. It was cool.'

Not so cool for Felton. 'Getting punched by Hermione – that one gets brought up a bit with me,' he admitted during an interview with MTV. 'A lot of street cred was lost on that film,' he sighed.

As well as filming at Leavesden Studios, the Potter crew took in a wide variety of locations around the UK to create the look of the film. St Paul's Cathedral in London and Virginia Water in Surrey were brought into play and the cast moved to the Highlands of Scotland for several weeks to film on purpose-built sets at Glencoe to bring Hagrid's hut and Hogwarts' Bridge to Nowhere to life. This was part of a deliberate attempt to highlight the 'Scottishness' of Potter in the third film. Although it's not explicit, there was a general understanding that Hogwarts was north of the border, so it was right to use the dramatic scenery of the Highlands. Unfortunately, no one bothered to mention the equally dramatic weather. 'Once we got to Scotland, it rained every day,' producer Mark Radcliffe told the *Making of The Prisoner of Azkaban* documentary. 'Literally the set would be washing out from under us. At lunch we had to have a helicopter dropping gravel, and have the crew put the gravel back in to keep the dirt from washing away from under the set. Then we'd have to bring everybody back in to try to work.'

As if to emphasise the fact that she was growing up, Emma's dressing-room door had a sign attached to it: 'Beware – Babe Inside'. For a more literal example, look no further than what happened to Emma on set on 15 April 2003, as recalled by actor Chris Rankin, who plays Percy Weasley. 'There was an apparent power cut in the middle of a huge piece of Emma's dialogue during a Great Hall scene,' he said in an interview with the BBC. 'We all thought, What's going on? And then 700 people burst into singing "Happy Birthday". It was all very nice, but I think she got embarrassed by it all.'

Meanwhile, Warner Brothers announced that the role of Dumbledore had been filled by Michael Gambon. The Dublin-born actor had been knighted in 1998 and had a staggering CV of theatre, television and stage work stretching back to the mid-1960s. Despite this, Gambon admitted to nerves on the first day of shooting. 'Having read the script, you get on set on the first morning, very frightened, and then I thought, How on earth am I going to play this part?' he admitted to the BBC. 'Then suddenly you get this feeling inside you, you've got the costume on, the wig, the beard, suddenly you've got long fingers like me, with gold rings, so the whole feeling and the image tells you how to play it.'

And Emma seemed happy with the choice. 'Obviously it's very hard to follow on from Richard Harris. He was a perfect Dumbledore. Michael did a really great job instead of trying to make himself look exactly like Richard Harris or try to copy him. He did his own thing with it and he's put a different spin on it. He's a more mischievous Dumbledore.'

Gambon proved his mischievous credentials early on by gleefully announcing that he had never read any of the Potter books – and had no intention of ever doing so. 'Well, I don't see any point,' he told *Empire* magazine. 'I've got the scripts. People who have read the books get miserable because of all the bits that have been cut out. So I just read the script. That's the best way. I just play him as myself. I don't ease myself into any role really. I stick a beard on and play me. Every part I play is just a variant of my own personality. No real character actor, of course, just me.'

The mischievous Gambon and the teenager-at-heart Cuarón were a deadly combination on set, proving that it wasn't just Emma and her co-stars who could use the set as their own personal playground.

'On my first Potter film, the director and I shoved a fart machine in Harry Potter's sleeping bag,' Gambon later explained to *Future Movies* about a scene where the pupils bed down in the Great Hall for protection against the 'murderous raving lunatic' Sirius Black. 'Daniel had his eye on one of the extra girls and asked, "Can she be in the next sleeping bag to me in this scene?" She was a beautiful girl playing a non-speaking part, so we agreed. I had the controller, and, as soon as he wakes up in the Great Hall, I pressed the button. It *destroyed* his credibility with her.'

Also joining the cast was Gary Oldman as Sirius Black, the shape-changing wizard who turns out to be Harry Potter's godfather. Radcliffe was thrilled by the casting of Oldman. The British actor had made a name playing tortured, morally suspect characters on screen, from Sid Vicious in Alex Cox's *Sid and Nancy* to Lee Harvey Oswald in *JFK*. He had a reputation for immersing himself totally in a role – even immersing himself further than was strictly healthy. Producer David Heyman said, 'Gary's an actor's actor, but also a producer's and a director's actor. He comes prepared, he's collaborative, he's passionate. I've heard the stories – "Oh, Gary . . ." – but nothing could be further from the truth. Gary is a hero. You just want to see him do it more. To have him flexing those not inconsiderable acting muscles in Harry Potter is a treat.'

As Sirius Black, Oldman was made to look like a wild-haired, tattooed heroin addict. 'I'm no stranger to the dark side,' he told Johnny Vaughn in an on-set interview. 'But really I'm playing a good guy. We *think* he's a bad guy. So I liked that dynamic, that twist at the end.'

Oldman was also full of praise for his young co-stars: 'Honestly, they really are fantastic kids. They're very professional. Very focused.'

Radcliffe for one idolised Oldman. Watson was less than impressed. To Radcliffe's horror, she had no idea who the multi-award-winning actor was, as she later explained during a press conference to promote the finished film. 'Dan almost bit my head off when he said, "Gary Oldman's been cast as Sirius Black." I said, "Who?" Now I know that's the most terrible thing that I could possibly say ever! Even though I didn't know him, he's great.'

Emma was slightly more impressed by some of the other casting decisions. 'Someone I was dying to work with was Emma Thompson, who got cast as the part of Professor Trelawney because I love her,' she said. 'She did a really great job. She is hilarious. I had really good fun with her because she was very creative and very involving with me. It was really flattering for her to involve me like that.'

For director Cuarón, it was Emma Watson and her young co-stars who ruled the roost. 'From my perspective,' he told the BBC, 'I found the grown-ups more intimidated by the kids. They'd done two movies, they are doing this movie, they are working every single day.'

For Emma, though, the reverse was true: the roll call of British acting talent that was scattered through the movie was a lot to deal with for an actress barely into her teens. 'The scene which had Alan Rickman [Severus Snape], Timothy Spall [Peter Pettigrew], Gary Oldman [Sirius Black] and David Thewlis [Remus Lupin] all in the same room was a bit overwhelming, but it was great because it really challenged me. Just watching them work was a huge help in terms of helping us mature as actors.'

With a brisk running time of 136 minutes – brisk by Potter standards, that is – *Prisoner of Azkaban* rattles along with fine set pieces such as the Dementors' invasion of the Hogwarts Express, a storm-lashed game of Quidditch and a werewolf finale where once again Hermione proves herself to be the bravest of the bunch.

The first surprise is seeing Emma's Hermione in her

'civilian' clothes as she bickers with Ron about their pets. It's hardly the stylish outfits that we were used to seeing Emma wearing at premieres and award ceremonies, but it was a start. 'It took me three films to get Hermione in jeans,' Emma told *USA Today*. 'To get out of the robes with the tights and the itchy jumpers. Whoo-hoo! [Being 13 is] different from 12 or 11. It's an archetypal age. Kids change so much. You want to change the way you dress, the way you look, the way you argue.'

When they get to Hogwarts the three stars look like typical teenagers at school: ties are askew, hair is messy and even Hermione has her shirt untucked. Director Cuarón wanted the film to have a more contemporary feel. Ron and Hermione argue constantly, but there's that pointer too about the way their relationship could head, as she awkwardly holds Ron's hand, while Harry tries to pet Buckbeak, the fearsome hippogriff. The moment is over in a second, but it was the kind of character detail that made the viewer warm to her. 'I feel quite close to Hermione,' Emma told the BBC. 'I feel very protective of her when I read the books, so I hope she ends up doing something that she loves. I hope she ends up being happy.' Could that mean Hermione being happy with Ron? 'Maybe! Maybe . . . if that makes her happy . . .'

There are noticeably longer takes, tracking shots and dialogue scenes involving the teenage stars than in previous films. Remember when Chris Columbus had to extend a shot in the edit (see chapter three) to make it look like Hermione and Harry had a lingering embrace? Sleight of hand like that was no longer required, because the three young actors stretched their acting abilities as their director stretched the length of takes he could capture. 'Basically, I think everything we learned with Chris, we were now able to put into practice with a different director,' Radcliffe told *Cinema Confidential*. 'I think the reason Alfonso was able to do longer takes and more complicated shots was because, with Chris, we didn't have the experience or the focus to do that kind of stuff. It is harder, it is more challenging, because we're getting older and if we're getting older and we're not being challenged there's no point in doing it really.'

There's a good running joke about Hermione seemingly appearing from nowhere during various points in the film. Cat lover Emma also gets to work with Crookshanks the cat: 'I loved working with that cat. He's so cute. He looks like he's been smashed in the face with a pan. He's so ugly, bless! But I love him. He's lovely and fluffy.'

Emma was even able to take her love of cats one step further this time around. 'I was given more unusual things to do,' she said, revelling in the expanded role the third film gave her. 'I become a cat in one scene! I loved that, because I have two cats at home.'

The burgeoning relationship between Hermione and Ron is key to the film: when they aren't arguing they're embracing. 'Any excuse to make out that they hate each other,' Emma said in an on-set interview for a 'making of' documentary. 'They're always niggling each other and having a go at each other. There's always this threat that they might actually like each other. And they don't like that at all.'

Then of course there's the famous Draco punch. 'That felt good,' Hermione says, summing up the audience feeling perfectly. In fact, we get to see the punch twice as Ms Granger takes the lead by going back in time and solving the mystery and saving the life of Buckbeak. *Prisoner of Azkaban* is Hermione's movie. 'Definitely! I love playing Hermione, she is so charismatic,' Emma told CBBC. 'She's a fantastic role to play, especially in this third one.'

'New boy' Michael Gambon – louder and showier than Richard Harris as Dumbledore – was full of praise for Emma and her young co-stars, in his own mischievous way: 'Awful, they are such bad actors! No, they are brilliant actors. The three of them are just the best. It was a joy to work with them, not one single iota of a problem. I remember, working in various scenes that I have with them, that they are so economical.'

Robbie Coltrane as Hagrid agreed. 'They're definitely getting older, they're not children any more,' he told the *Daily Mail*. 'They're not quite as moody as adolescents. They are fantastic, I don't know how they manage. They're on set longer than anyone else is.'

Director Alfonso Cuarón seemed to save his most lavish praise for Emma. 'If she decided, she could have a big career,' he told *The Times*. 'She's growing up so beautifully. I'd love to work with her again, away from Harry Potter. She listens intensely, and there's an intelligence and warmth about her.'

The world premiere of *Prisoner of Azkaban* took place on 23 May 2004 at the Radio City Music Hall in New

York. Emma wore a strapless silvery beige dress with her hair in ringlets as she posed for photos and spoke to reporters about Hermione's role in the film. 'In the first two films, people were mean to her, teasing her, being rude to her, and she's always taking it, pretending she didn't hear, saying, "Oh, no, let's just forget about it." But in this one she's, like, "No, that's it, I'm not taking any more, I'm going to fight back," and she punches Draco, storms out on her teachers. She's rock and roll!'

At a press conference the day after the New York premiere, Emma would make her first really eye-catching public fashion statement. She'd celebrated her 13th birthday on set, but now she was a confident 14-year-old. As she and Daniel talked at a top table with US journalists, the two teenagers were a study in contrasts: Radcliffe wore a plain white T-shirt; Watson, on the other hand, wore a red and gold *Sgt. Pepper*-style military jacket. Not only were the film journalists taking note of Emma Watson, the fashion writers had started to as well.

For the London premiere six days later at the Odeon Leicester Square, Emma styled her hair up and wore a flowing purple dress – purple was a recurring sartorial theme for the young actress – along with matching purple shoes and a white corsage. J. K. Rowling later made a point of saying in a posting on her website how striking Emma looked. 'The premiere was fun, as always,' she wrote. 'It was the first time I had met Gary Oldman, David Thewlis and Michael Gambon, all of whom do a really magnificent job in the film. And it was, as ever, great to see Dan, Rupert and Emma, who get taller and better looking (and in Emma's case, more beautiful) every time I see them.' In Rowling's view, Emma, Rupert and Daniel were also 'miraculously, the most grounded, least egotistical teenage actors you are ever likely to meet'.

Photographers and fans went into overdrive when they spotted Emma and Daniel briefly holding hands as they waited to have their picture taken by the massed ranks of the press covering the premiere. Camera flashes crackled into life to capture the moment that would keep the Internet rumour-merchants busy for some weeks to come. 'I'm having a pretty good time as a teenager at the moment,' she told journalists. 'It's an interesting age. It's a time of discovery, of making mistakes and learning from them. I intend to enjoy it.'

But would the critics enjoy the film to the same extent? There would always be doubters, but *Prisoner of Azkaban* seemed to hit the spot for most reviewers and the reason for the franchise's new lease on life was clear. 'Bringing in Mexican-born Cuarón to replace Chris Columbus for this third instalment of the Potter franchise has, on the whole, proved a success,' said *Time Out*. 'Though flawed, it's the most interesting movie of the three. Compared to its predecessors, this is a more wintry, thoughtful and rewarding movie.'

Entertainment Weekly was also keen to flag up the influence that Cuarón has brought to the film: 'Shot in spooky gradations of silver and shadow, *Prisoner of Azkaban* is the first movie in the series with fear and wonder in its bones, and genuine fun, too.'

As was becoming increasingly common, it was Emma

who was singled out for particular praise – and sometimes the praise bordered on the gushing: 'Every now and again you see an actress so young and gifted that she makes one take pause,' said the influential *Ain't It Cool News* movie website. 'As she continues to mature in this series, I think there will be not a single boy or adult male that doesn't have a schoolboy crush on her. She is a lady of the highest order.'

The lady in question was doing her best to remain grounded, not easy in the face of such overwhelming attention. 'You know, I still fall out with my brother, I still have to make my bed, I still see my friends,' she said. 'I try to lead a really normal life. Basically, the only way that it's changed is what I'm doing in everyday life.'

Along with the rave reviews, there was also the grinding round of press interviews that Emma undertook with her usual good grace. Among the usual questions – 'Do you have a boyfriend?'; 'Do you have a crush on Dan or Rupert?'; 'What magical power would you like to have?' – a new theme started to appear. Not only was she giving no guarantees that she was going to appear in all the remaining Potter films, but she wasn't even prepared to commit herself to being an actress. 'I feel incredibly lucky to have been given the opportunity to have been in such a fantastic film. I mean, my ambitions could not have even *dreamed* of the scale and greatness that Harry Potter is,' she told journalists at the New York premiere of the film. 'But I love performing and being creative. There are so many different aspects of the film world, that, even if I don't pursue the acting, there's something else I'm bound to end up doing. I'm just going to go with the flow and see what happens.'

Emma Watson was now asserting her independence. *She* would decide what her future held – and, when she had made that decision, she'd let us know. From now on, it was 'one film at a time'.

The team behind the Potter films admitted that there were no guarantees as to how many – if any – of the young stars would see out the whole series. 'There may come a day when the kids make a decision that they want to move on, but we haven't reached that point yet,' producer David Heyman told the *Mirror*. 'In the books the children continue to grow. So by the seventh book they will be 17 or 18 and so will Daniel, Rupert and Emma.'

Of the trio, Emma was the most difficult to pin down in terms of her future plans. 'I love art. I love being on stage, singing, dancing,' she told *The Times*. 'So even if I don't end up acting, maybe I'll try screenwriting, whatever gets thrown at me.' One thing she was sure about: the serious-minded, career-driven path taken by her parents was something that held no interest for her. 'I can't really see myself in an office,' she said.

FIVE

HERMIONE IS TOTALLY SWEPT OFF HER FEET

In November 2004, the nature of Emma Watson's fame came full circle. In London's Oxford Street, thousands of children stood in the cold waiting for a glimpse of the teenage actress as she switched on this shopping Mecca's Christmas lights. With a woolly scarf to keep her warm – purple, of course – Emma did the honours along with the athletes there to promote London's bid for the 2012 Olympic Games and popera stars Il Divo. Emma was there essentially to plug the DVD release of *Prisoner of Azkaban*. The podium was festooned with images from the DVD cover and the lights had a Potter theme. She also took the trouble to tell the crowd she would really like a candy-floss machine for Christmas.

The event stirred memories of being in the same street eight years earlier, but that time Emma was in the crowd and it was her pop heroines who had been the guests of honour. 'I've wanted to do it ever since I was very young and I saw the Spice Girls do it,' she told the BBC. 'I love Oxford Street. I've come here most Christmases because I love the lights and all the beautiful displays in all the shops.'

For a teenager who talked constantly about the 'girl power' demonstrated by the character of Hermione Granger, it must have brought home how much things had changed, flicking the same switch the Spice Girls had done when she was just five. It clearly made a profound impact on her. Despite all the other astonishing experiences that had come her way, she would later describe the switch-on as the highlight of her year. 'I will remember that for the rest of my life,' she said.

Emma spent the winter taking in another new experience – skiing. It was something she'd wanted to do for some time, but, as with so many things in her young life, she was prevented from doing so because of contractual obligations to the Potter franchise. However, because of the way the next film had been scheduled, for the first time since she was nine, Emma had a temporary taste of freedom, as she explained to showbiz writer Maria Morreale: 'The brilliant thing is that this year, because of the big enough gap between the third and the fourth [films], it would mean that if I did break my leg I'd be all right before we started filming again.'

A broken limb clearly wasn't causing her any sleepless nights, but her forthcoming exams clearly were: 'I looked at a GCSE book the other day and I was like, "Oh my God, I'm never going to pass!" It's just like it goes on for ever and ever and ever, and the amount of work is a bit like, *aagh*!'

To make things worse for her, the split-schooling schedule of between being educated on set and taking classes at Headington School was causing some confusion – she didn't actually know what subjects she was taking. 'I'm not actually really sure,' she said. 'I think you have to do maths; you have to do physics, chemistry, biology. I think you have to take English, and I think you have to take French. And then I've got stuff like Latin, Spanish, geography, history.'

After her holiday, Emma returned – with both legs thankfully intact – to start work on the next instalment of the franchise, *Harry Potter and the Goblet of Fire*. J. K. Rowling's book of the same name had been released in summer 2000 with a barrage of PR hoopla, including a full-size Hogwarts Express that took Rowling on a promotional tour of Britain.

In Book Four, Harry is given a series of seemingly impossible tasks to carry out as part of the Triwizard Tournament, a competition between wizarding schools that he has been entered into initially without his knowledge. Harry's name is produced out of the Goblet of Fire, despite being too young to enter. He finally comes face to face with 'He Who Must Not Be Named', Lord Voldemort, during the final challenge, resulting in the murder of one of the key characters, Cedric Diggory. Much was made on the book's release about this impending death, causing great concern among young readers that one of the main three characters was about to make a violent exit. The story itself had been the most difficult for Rowling to conjure up. 'Book Four nearly caused me a nervous breakdown,' Rowling told the *Daily Mirror*. 'I sailed straight into the writing of it, having just finished *Azkaban*. I had written what I thought at the time was half the book – it turns out now to have been about a third. And I realised there was this big hole in the middle of the plot and I had to go back and unpick and redo. That's part of the reason it's longer than I thought it was going to be. On Book Four I was working ten-hour days.'

Those ten-hour days produced a 636-page monster of a book – nearly 100 more in the US edition (because of typographical and design considerations). It was so big that the producers first investigated the possibility of splitting it into two films. 'We went through the process of thinking about that, of thinking, Was there enough here for two films?' producer David Heyman told *Empire* magazine. 'Where would you break this if you were to do two films? Were there two coherent stories within it? We came to the conclusion that it would work very well as one film.'

The next problem was finding a new director. Alfonso Cuarón had decided that one film was enough. His replacement was Mike Newell, director of films such as *Four Weddings and Funeral*, *Dance with a Stranger* and *Donnie Brasco*. Newell would be the first British director of this most British of stories. 'It was very daunting to start with,' Newell later told the BBC. 'The book is as big as a house brick and one is unsure how to attack it. Little by little you lose your terror of it.'

Producer David Heyman recalled, 'I thought it would be nice to have a British director. This book is the funniest, or has the potential to be the funniest, and Mike had shown in *Four Weddings* a great sense of humour. There is also a thriller aspect to this, and, when you look at *Donnie Brasco* and the darkness of *Dance with a Stranger*, he has ability there. And he had worked with children. Those were the governing reasons.'

'I have a lot of respect for Mike,' Emma told the BBC's *Newsround* when asked about the new director. 'I genuinely think he's brilliant. He's so creative and he's so passionate about making this the best film, and he won't settle for anything else.'

With a new director came new techniques that the young performers had to adapt to. Mike Newell's idea of breaking the ice among the young stars caused a few raised eyebrows – the director decided that wrestling was the best way forward. 'I didn't want them to think of me as an authority figure,' he explained to journalists at a press conference to launch the finished film. 'They had grown up to the point where they had a lot to give. So I had a fight with one of the Weasley twins in a bid to lose my dignity. They wouldn't see me as an authority figure if I was rolling around in the dust with a 17-year-old!'

Alfonso Cuarón's 'write an essay about your character' idea went out of the window and in came improvisational workshops. A 'bonding week' was organised so that new cast members could integrate with the existing young team. 'Mike Newell brought all of the actors together and asked us to improvise love scenes,' Emma later told *Bravo*. 'I was appalled. I was so humiliated, but then I saw that everyone else made a fool of themselves. Now I am not afraid to make a fool of myself.'

Among the new arrivals who were sent to make fools of themselves alongside Emma and friends was 18-year-old Robert Pattinson, a London-born model and actor who was just starting out on his career when he got the call about playing the role of Cedric Diggory. 'I was shooting another film in South Africa during the entire period of the casting process for *Goblet of Fire* [the rather silly, made-for German-TV dragon-slayer 'epic' *Sword of Xanten*]. The casting agent had contacted my agent about seeing me for Cedric. Basically, I was able to get a meeting with Mike Newell and two of the casting directors the day before I left for South Africa to shoot this other movie. It was before anyone else had been seen for the other parts, so it was quite a cool position to be in. They did the rest of the casting for it afterwards. Then, the day I returned from South Africa, I got the call-back and they told me in the audition that I had got the part.'

Pattinson's first task was to muck in with the improvisational tasks that he and the other teen stars had been set. He was immediately impressed by Emma Watson: 'Emma just *does it*,' he later told the IESB movie website. 'She's an *actress* and she always has been. She's just an incredibly intelligent young person. Very impressive.'

Pattinson's worldwide fame with the *Twilight* films was still three years away, but Emma spotted that he was the total movie-star package from that first meeting during bonding week. 'He was always very intelligent, nice, talented, good-looking,' she later explained to MTV. 'He kinda had everything *there*.'

Daniel Radcliffe would later describe the atmosphere on set among the teenage actors at this time as 'unbelievably horny'. He told *Esquire* magazine, 'There was a period when we were the only boys and girls any of us knew. And so, you know, we were all unbelievably horny from about the third film to probably about the end of the fifth; then it all settled down. But, God, for a few years . . . There was never anybody I fancied that much in the cast, though the conspiracy theorists always like to say that me and Emma are dating. We know it'd be everything the fans ever wanted. I'm sorry, guys, it's not happening. It's just not. There's something really incestuous about the idea of it.'

By way of response to Radcliffe's comments, Emma pointed out that they were far from being the only boys she saw: there were plenty of them in and around Oxford. Radcliffe's comments would be pounced upon as yet another hint or clue that there was something more than friendship between the young stars. 'Dan Radcliffe is very charming, and very, very sweet,' she said. 'We've been handling this situation for six years now. Everyone has been going, "Are you and Dan together?" Because it doesn't happen in the books, everyone is so desperate for it to happen in real life that any opportunity to come up with a story about it is taken.'

As ever, the pool of acting talent involved in the Potter world was deepened with yet more, established performers joining the team for the new film. Among them were Dublin-born actor Brendan Gleeson as new Defence

Against the Dark Arts teacher Alastor 'Mad Eye' Moody and Ralph Fiennes as Lord Voldemort. 'Ralph Fiennes was certainly on my wish list from the first moment we started working on Potter,' producer Heyman told *Premiere* magazine. 'If it is ever not possible, generally it is to do with availability. These are long shoots, and sometimes we need actors for long periods of time and they have other commitments – they do theatre as well. We have been very lucky. I don't think Ralph was a fan of the books in that sense. He is a thoughtful and considered man, he read and he thought and went through the part with Mike and after that meeting he was on board. They feel very comfortable with each other and how the interpretation of Voldemort should be. Then it was just about making a deal. That is a natural process.'

Fiennes had form in playing evil characters: the serial killer the Tooth Fairy in *Red Dragon* and Nazi commandant Amon Göth in Steven Spielberg's Holocaust drama *Schindler's List*. For *Goblet of Fire* what was required was total evil. 'That was one of the blessings of a part like this, where you're meant to be playing the distillation of evil, whatever that is. Which can be anything, so I got a lot of takes. I think the one thing, if anything, was a sort of question of unpredictability in him, so no one quite knows what he's gonna do next or say next. Which I hope makes him slightly sort of dangerous.'

There was also the matter of making Fiennes look like an evil, noseless Dark Lord. 'The shaved head, the weird translucent skin – we wanted it to be simple, with a simple gown,' Fiennes later told the TV show *Inside the Actors Studio*. 'Then the question of the nose came up. I was a bit neurotic about whether it would work or not. When I saw it, I was very happy with it.'

Miranda Richardson was cast as another dangerous character, conniving journalist Rita Skeeter, the *Daily Prophet*'s most poisonous hack with a suspiciously inside track on all things Potter-related. Skeeter paints a picture of Hermione in her articles as a glorified wizard groupie: she is 'plain but ambitious'.

Richardson had worked with Mike Newell before on *Dance with a Stranger* and *Enchanted April*. But there was one other role that Richardson had tackled that could have caused problems for her when she arrived on set. In 2003, Richardson had taken part in a Harry Potter spoof for Comic Relief called *Harry Potter and the Secret Chamberpot of Azerbaijan*. During the pitiless send-up, Jennifer Saunders played a ludicrously gurning Rupert Grint, Dawn French was an unfeasibly large-chested Daniel Radcliffe and Basil Brush was Dobby. Richardson was Emma Watson, over-enunciating her way through an interview. 'A lot of people think I must be really like my character,' lisps Richardson in a curly Hermione wig. 'But I'm not. It's different. That's acting. Hermione's certainly not like me.'

Cut to Richardson as Hermione – behaving *exactly* the same as Richardson as Emma.

When she turned up for her first day on set as Rita Skeeter, Richardson was worried that the young actress might have taken offence. 'I was a bit nervous of Emma,'

Richardson told journalist Jeff Dawson in 2005. 'I thought she might say, "I'm not like that!"'

Emma had the good grace not to make a scene; it could have been worse if the uncensored version of the Comic Relief sketch had gone out: "My last line was, "Are you looking at my Snitch?"" Richardson recalled. 'But they wouldn't let it go out on the air, and I was very sad about that.'

Filming for Movie Number Four took place at Pinewood Studios in Buckinghamshire, Beachy Head in East Sussex and Evanton near Inverness in the Scottish Highlands. As ever, Harry Potter headquarters at Leavesden Studios was a home from home. Along with existing sets featuring the Great Hall, the Quidditch stadium and the wizarding village of Hogsmeade, a major addition to the set was a giant water tank – believed to be the biggest in Europe – built especially for underwater fight sequences with the 'merpeople'.

With such an enormous source book to cram into one film, it was inevitable that some aspects of the plot would have to go. 'Inevitably you kill off some darlings' was David Heyman's slightly luvvie-ish explanation for the cuts during an interview with *Premiere* magazine. 'This was the longest book so far, and there are things that I love that we can't have. Again, we have taken out elements that don't relate as directly to Harry and Harry's journey.'

One casualty was a delightful subplot involving Hermione and her battle to improve the lot of one of Rowling's most downtrodden creations. 'Yeah, SPEW [Society for the Protection of Elfish Welfare] which is the whole Hermione-fighting-for-the-rights-of-the-house-elves bit,' Heyman said. 'It is funny, but it doesn't relate to Harry's story. So it falls by the wayside.'

As Heyman had hoped, *Harry Potter and the Goblet of Fire* is indeed a reassuringly British affair, and many scenes have a grimy, postwar look to them. Emma's Hermione acts as a go-between, negotiating the teenage head-butting of Ron and Harry, despite pointing out that she is not an owl (the preferred message carriers at Hogwarts) when asked to pass on one message too many. She's even caught in a clinch with Harry by Rita Skeeter. But it's two new young men who really catch her eye. There's Viktor Krum (Stanislav Ianevski), the 'best Quidditch seeker in the world', according to Ron, and ruddy-faced 'strapping lad' Cedric Diggory (Robert Pattinson). The future *Twilight* star – who would go on to play vampire Edward Cullen in the cult American franchise – makes his entrance by jumping out of a tree. 'Very manly' was Emma's appraisal of Pattinson's look for the film. 'Rugged and dirty . . . it's good!'

'Everyone was going pretty crazy over him when *Harry Potter* was released,' Emma later told *Access Hollywood* when asked about Pattinson's breakthrough role in the film. 'He's quite eccentric, he's very funny. He reads a lot, he writes a lot. He's a cool guy.'

Despite the epic Quidditch sequences, mid-air dragon battles and underwater monsters, the stand-out section of the film didn't involve fancy digital effects or intense battle scenes – just a simple walk down some stairs. The scene is the Christmas Eve Yule Ball – an opportunity for some 'well-mannered frivolity', according to Professor Minerva McGonagall (Maggie Smith). There is the usual jockeying for dates among the students, the kind you'd see in any teen movie. Neither Ron nor Harry has asked Hermione – a big mistake, when they clap eyes on her. 'That's the thing I loved doing,' she told MTV. 'Because I can relate, in so many ways, to her situation and what's happening to her. How insensitive boys can be, how awkward it can be. It's always that boy who's mean to you and teases you who's actually the guy who has the huge crush on you.'

With her hair styled half up and half down and wearing a stunning pink satin dress, Emma/Hermione finally gets to shed the tatty jumpers and ratty hairdos and *shine* as she walks down the steps to enter the ball. 'That dress! I felt such pressure, I cannot even begin to tell you,' she later told fans on her official website. 'This was Hermione's big reveal where she goes from being perceived as just bookish and nerdy to being beautiful. It's the moment I suppose when Ron finally sees what he's missing. But I remember being terrified I'd fall down the stairs, everyone was watching me!'

Emma's face when Krum clicks his heels, bows and takes her hand is worth the price of admission in itself. 'It was,' she said, 'a duckling-into-swan kind of moment.'

Emma had previously said that *Pretty Woman*, starring Julia Roberts, was one of her favourite films. In one key scene, Roberts makes quite an entrance in a striking red dress. Now Emma had been given a scene-stealing entrance of her own. 'It was amazing actually,' she told *The Early Show* in 2005. 'To some extent, I always played down the way I looked in the films. Suddenly, they really wanted this kind of Julia Roberts *Pretty Woman*-esque moment. It was beautiful and for this scene you had to learn to waltz, which was fantastic. All the cast was involved. It was great.'

Stanislav Ianevski – who'd never acted professionally before – was suitably bullish about the dancing scenes, as befits a young man playing a heroic Quidditch player. 'I think we made a great dancing couple,' he said in an interview with the Scholastic website. 'I enjoyed it a lot and I hope she enjoyed it as well. It was very good. Yes, we had lessons where we were taught the different dances. It was quite tough at first, but, once we got into them, we were really one of the best couples there.'

Emma explained, 'Hermione is totally swept off her feet and that's nice. She doesn't know what's happening to her.'

In fact, Emma is seen waltzing for only a few brief moments, but she had clearly been bitten by the dancing bug and even fancied showing off her skills on a well-known TV competition. 'I'm desperate to be on [BBC1's] *Strictly Come Dancing*,' she said. 'The best bit about doing the new Harry Potter movie was that I got to learn how to waltz and now I've fallen in love with ballroom dancing. I don't know if they will ask me to come and do it – I guess we'll have to see what they think of my moves in the film.'

More time is given to her bopping to a rock band led by Pulp singer Jarvis Cocker. Krum's courting of Hermione shocks the other two main characters – it certainly gets Ron's 'wand in knot'. 'I thought the introduction of romance in what is a much darker film and this kind of awkwardness between boys and girls makes up for quite a lot of the humour,' Emma told *Newsround*. 'I think it's great. Stanislav was a really nice guy, genuinely a really, really nice guy. We had a lot of fun learning to dance, it was great.'

Despite all the razzle-dazzle of the effects sequences, it was this moment that caught many of the reviewers' attention when the film was released in November 2005. 'Harry and Ron find themselves furious, confused and resentful to see that Hermione scrubs up into a premier-league babe and is being squired by the young foreign wizard superstar,' said the *Guardian*. 'But she'd accepted his invitation only because she was sick of waiting for either of these two dullards (particularly Ron) to do the decent thing and invite her. Hermione is angry and heartbroken at their churlish sneering, and Emma Watson's gutsy, confident performance nicely shows that inside and outside the world of magic there is a growing discrepancy between a teenage girl's status and her accelerating emotional and intellectual development.'

'An unexpectedly black and at times very frightening foray into the less fun side of wizardry and magic,' said the *Telegraph*. 'Hermione (Emma Watson), meanwhile, takes her nose out of magic books long enough to doll herself up in makeup and ball gown and to such lovely effect that she even takes Ron's breath away.'

The *Daily Mail* agreed: 'Emma Watson's studious Hermione comes into her own at the fabulous Christmas Ball, which provides a breather after the first task, in which Harry does battle with a fearsome Hungarian Horntail dragon in a gripping sequence that will have small fry ducking for cover.'

In fact, there was so much concern about how small fry would react to the film that it was decided to give it a 12A rating, meaning that children under 12 couldn't see the film without a grown-up. 'You can really spot the differences in the four films,' Helen Pang of the British Board of Film Classification explained. 'The first one, *Harry Potter and the Philosopher's Stone*, was classified back in October 2001 and Harry and his friends were so sweet and innocent then. As the characters have become teenagers and are more experienced in magic, the tone of the films has become darker, the moments of intensity more frequent and there are far fewer jokes and lighter moments. The result is that this is the first Harry Potter film at 12A. Be prepared for a very different film to the first three!'

Although it could limit the access that young fans had to the film – maybe even affect its box-office performance – Emma agreed with the censors' decision: 'The audience who were the first fans of Harry Potter have grown up with the films. We may have lost some of the much younger audience, but I'm in it and I was scared! This book is much more of a thriller than it has ever been before. The films have always been about being faithful to the books and we cannot avoid the fact that someone dies in it. They have made something that is true to the book.'

So Emma's entrance at the Yule Ball created a stir, but so did her appearance at the film's London premiere on 6 November 2005. EMMA OUTSHINES STARS AT POTTER PREMIERE, proclaimed the headline in the *Daily Mail*, claiming that the young actress was the centre of attention rather than star guests such as Rob Lowe, Kate Beckinsale and Madonna, although the Material Girl admitted she'd never read any of Rowling's books. Emma created even more excitement among the crowd and the press than the caged, fire-breathing dragon that had been set up outside the cinema. 'At 15, she has not had many years to refine her public image,' the *Mail* gushed. 'But Emma Watson proved she could grab the limelight just as effectively as Madonna as she arrived for the premiere of *Harry Potter and the Goblet of Fire*. Miss Watson, who plays Hermione Granger, looked every inch the movie star as she sashayed down the red carpet in Leicester Square.'

Emma was dressed in a striking embroidered white gown, white headband and gold slippers; again, she had showed she was a fashionista to watch. What's more, the outfit was a dress with a backstory. 'I looked everywhere for the perfect dress and then I found this vintage 1920s dress in a shop in Notting Hill and I fell in love with it,' she told reporters. 'But what's amazing is that I've since discovered it was specially made for a 1920s screen goddess, which makes it even more appropriate.'

At the time, Emma drew a discreet veil over the actual story behind the dress until the full details were known. The dress had actually belonged to another child star, Anna May Wong, who started in films aged 13. Her first picture was the 1919 melodrama *The Red Lantern*. After her initial success as a teenager, Anna May had then carved out a career for herself as a vampish seductress.

She died in 1961. Emma had bought the dress from an antiques shop in Notting Hill run by Virginia Bates, who told the *Sunday Telegraph* that the damaged garment had brought to her by the late actress's maid. 'It was her who revealed that the dress belonged to Anna May,' she said. 'Anna May's personal maid had lived with her in Hollywood and when the actress died her maid was given several of her personal effects. It was handmade and in those days they had their own seamstress, so there is no designer. They would have seen something in Paris and used that as a blueprint for a dress which Anna May probably only wore once.'

Despite what many people expected, Emma got no assistance when it came to choosing premiere outfits. 'Everyone imagines there were stylists on tap from the studio, but we got nothing,' she later told journalist Lisa Armstrong. 'Sometimes I had two days' notice before an event and there was nothing appropriate for a 14-year-old to wear. I'd look in my wardrobe and . . . literally, nothing. It was either borrow from my stepmother or go to the bridesmaid department of Harrods.'

J. K. Rowling's sixth Potter book – *Harry Potter and the Half-Blood Prince* – had been released less than four months earlier, so many of the journalists' questions were about the future of the franchise and in particular the next film – the fifth – *Harry Potter and the Order of the Phoenix*. 'Every film takes, like, a year to do and the six months after that is all the production, so you kind of have to take it one film at a time because otherwise it's a bit overwhelming,' Emma told reporters. 'But I can tell you that I'm back in February for the fifth film. I'm on for the fifth, I know that much.'

Producer David Heyman confirmed that there would be changes: 'It starts filming in February. We asked Mike [Newell] if he would do it and he said no. These films are real endurance tests and I don't know how Chris Columbus managed to do two back to back. At the end of each film we ask the director if they want to do the next one. We asked Alfonso [Cuarón] to do the fourth and he said no and Mike said no to the fifth. We've hired someone called David Yates, who is a brilliant director. He directed *State of Play*, *Girl in the Café* and *Sex Traffic*. I think we've been really lucky. Each director has been just right for the film they've done and I think David Yates is the right director for the fifth film.'

For her part – four films in and with a fifth just round the corner – Emma was as comfortable with the red-carpet experience as she was with playing the part that had made her famous. But maybe, as in Miranda Richardson's spoof of Emma in *Harry Potter and the Secret Chamberpot of Azerbaijan*, Emma and Hermione were now one and the same. 'It felt like I didn't have to act at times,' she admitted. 'I know Hermione so well. There's so much of her in me, and me in her. It's been wonderful and I'm very fond of Hermione's character. She's turning into someone that people can identify with and she's a great role model.'

There were veiled suggestions in some parts of the press that Emma had been 'worse for wear' after the *Goblet of Fire* premiere – a surprising claim to be made about anyone with such a squeaky-clean, sensible reputation. What's more, it was claimed that she and the other Potter stars were contractually obliged to keep on the straight and narrow, something she has since denied: 'I've never seen a "good behaviour" clause – I honestly think that's a myth – but I actually wouldn't ever need one. It's just not necessary. Daniel, Rupert and I have been incredibly protected doing the Harry Potter movies. There seems to be this feeling that all of us were bursting to break out of these images we had created, but that's never been the case. We all share the same view. None of us court celebrity, none of us want to be part of the game. I'm not tempted by parties or drugs. I don't actually like being drunk, particularly in public.'

Boozing to someone of her background just wasn't a big deal. 'I was never *not* allowed alcohol,' she explained to the *Sunday Times*. 'I was seven when I had my first glass of wine, mixed with water and with a meal. I found it really strange when I got to school and everyone was like, "Ooh, we've got alcohol!' I wasn't interested.'

But the press were very interested indeed when pictures of Emma apparently guzzling beer from a bottle appeared on the Internet several months later. In one of the snaps, Emma could be seen at a restaurant table with a bottle of Corona tilted to her lips, pulling a rather self-conscious 'Ooh, I've got alcohol' kind of face. The feature writers had a field day with 'Emma goes off the rails' stories. Eventually, Emma answered the critics. 'Well, it was kind of frustrating because I wasn't even drinking,' she told *Sugar*. 'I was posing as a joke! But it's awkward, because there's the story there – "She's going to be an alcoholic". Then they bring out the whole screwed-up-child-star thing. It's when something that innocent is turned into something so serious. I did think, Be more careful. But I never want to get to a point where I feel I can't live my life. There's a balance, definitely.'

It was nothing more than any teenager would be likely to get up to – and Emma seemed to be going through a fairly typical teenage experience at this stage in her life, despite her fame. Mum Jacqueline could – in Emma's words – be 'fearsome' and would be the parent most likely to provide punishment. If there was conflict to be found inside the complex series of relationships in the extended Watson family, it tended to be between mother and daughter.

'Lots of opinions at both sets of parents' houses' was Emma's brother Alex's appraisal of his sister's teen-angst period. 'Emma wasn't any more bratty than any other teenager, but she and Mum definitely had lots of debates – that would be a good euphemism.'

At this stage, Emma was on £50-a-month pocket money from her dad Chris. 'He still gives me a monthly allowance,' she said. 'He insists! And, to be honest, I appreciate that. It makes me feel more normal. He really helps me because he doesn't want me to live this completely different, crazy life. I'm not spoilt.'

When the figure was later reported in the press, it was misquoted as £50 a *week*, rather than the more modest real amount. Although she was blissfully unaware of it, she was now a *seriously* wealthy young woman. 'By the

third or fourth film, the money was starting to get . . .
serious,' Emma told *Vogue* magazine in 2010. 'I had
no idea.'

SIX

EMMA DOESN'T WANT TO DO IT ANY MORE

The idea of starting the next Potter in February 2006 turned out to be an overly optimistic one. All three of the young leads had signed on the dotted line to do it, Emma Watson, it's believed, being the last to agree, having thought long and hard about it first. But the education of two of the teenagers would get in the way of production. The press reported that it would cost Warner Brothers £2 million to put a freeze on production while Emma and Daniel took their exams: GCSEs for Emma and AS for Daniel.

Emma applied her usual work ethic to the task of passing her exams – but she did allow herself one break to mark a certain milestone. In April, more than 150 people – including Rupert Grint – turned out for her 16th birthday party, held at Hertford College, part of Oxford University. They sang Happy Birthday to her in the college's 15th-century courtyard before getting stuck in at the bar – and realising that they had to pay for their own drinks. This was part of Emma's plan to avoid the event turning too messy, since non-alcoholic drinks such as 'Hermione Hangovers' and 'Wicked Watsons' were free. Despite the good intentions, the *Sun* gleefully alleged that Emma had been spotted 'knocking back' beer, dancing to The Prodigy and being 'all over' a boy at the end of the night.

Press speculation about Emma and the opposite sex had been fairly circumspect up until this stage. She believed that boys avoided her because of who she was, or made fun of her to show off to their mates. Also, much of her life was spent on film sets, where most of the youngest available males were ten years her senior. 'That's my problem,' she said. 'I think, Yeah, he's really good-looking, but he's, like, 25! Come on, help me out here! So, no, that's not really happening. People say to me, "Oh it must be so easy for you, boys must be lining up for you." It's really not easy. It's really not. I suppose guys are . . . kind of intimidated by me and have their defences up. It's a minefield, to be quite honest with you. Really. Ugh! It's stressful. I really like guys as friends, actually. I have about as many guy friends as girlfriends, which is kind of unusual, I suppose. But, because I'm in these films, there tend to be more guys around than girls. Plus, you know, I spend so much time here [on set]. So, yeah. I will just have to wait. Maybe someone will find me. We'll see.'

According to the press, someone did find her. It appeared that Emma's 16th birthday marked a major shift in the way she was treated by the tabloid press. They were desperate for her to grow up and yet wanted her to remain a child for ever. 'Like Peter Pan, yeah, I think they do,' she said. 'I think it's going to take a while to shake off the British press. Every headline I'm in, there is some reference to magic or broomsticks or witches or whatever! So it will take a while. The books and the films are loved so much that people don't want to let go, they don't want it to end but unfortunately I'm growing up, I'm not gonna be young for ever.'

She was becoming more of a target for paparazzi, and being 'papped' was all part of the game for many young actresses. But Emma was different. 'To be honest, I don't really court them,' she said when asked about being snapped in the street. 'I don't really encourage them. If I know they'll be somewhere, then I choose not to go there. I live in Oxford, and they're too lazy, luckily, to get their butts down to Oxford, so I'm usually fine a lot of the time. And when I'm in London I live a very low-profile life. Really. I don't choose to go to a lot of events where I know that they'll be there. I kind of just avoid them, really.'

But now she was 16. In the eyes of the press, it seemed she was fair game in a previously no-go area: her love life. 'I love someone who can make me laugh, who makes me feel I can be myself around them,' she told the *Sydney Morning Herald*, when asked the inevitable question: what kind of boys do you like? 'Confidence is good; arrogance is not. Someone I can really talk to, who doesn't bore me, is genuine, just interesting. Someone I can relax with. You have such high expectations. The other way you can look at it is that, if I list a lot of attributes, then I'm sort of widening my scope. You don't have to have all the attributes – just one or two will suffice.'

It was as if journalists waited for her to become 16 before rubbing their hands and declaring open season. Before long, she was being linked to the first in a series of young men: rugby player Tom Ducker from Chipping Norton in Oxfordshire, also 16. Again, it was the *Sun* that first linked the two, claiming Ducker – who'd recently been signed up by the London Wasps Academy in a scheme to develop young players – was a 'real-life Victor Krum'. 'Harry Potter star Emma Watson is dating a rugby ace,' the paper said. 'Emma, 16, has been on a string of nights out with strapping Tom Ducker, also 16. He is regarded as such a rising star that he has been signed up by the elite Wasps Academy. Emma – better known as Hermione in the hit films – was spotted sitting on his knee at a party. A source said: "They began dating last September and are very cosy with each other." Emma recently complained she was finding it difficult to find a boyfriend.'

Emma's approach to the stories about her and Ducker – and about future romances – would be a consistent one: none of your business. 'I wouldn't tell you if I did have a boyfriend,' she said to the *Daily Mail*, when asked if she was in a relationship, 'as it would be unfair to the other person.'

Slightly more willing to talk was Ali Abdelhafidh, owner of the Castel Plage restaurant on the Promenade des Anglais near Nice. The couple had booked into the

Château de la Chevre d'Or in nearby Eze and were spotted out on the town drinking champagne and eating lobsters. 'They were clearly loving each other's company and said they were in a very romantic place, with the Mediterranean just in front of them and great music,' Abdelhafidh told the *Daily Mail*. 'They said they were having a wonderful holiday and did not leave until well after 2am. It was great to see a young couple so much in love but Emma had time for everyone else, too. A lot of celebrities come here, including Elton John and Bono, but having Emma here was something special. She's a real star in every sense of the word.'

Emma was photographed next to a piece of artwork that caught her eye, a black-and-white piece with the words '*Je suis incognito ici, faites le savoir*' in scrolled writing. Tellingly, the words translate as 'I am incognito here, tell everybody'. 'Emma fell in love with it and offered to buy it there and then,' Ali Abdelhafidh told the paper. 'The words on the piece seemed to sum up her evening. But sadly it just wasn't for sale, so she posed for a photo next to the picture instead.'

Ducker's father John was quickly tracked down by journalists to give his view of the reported romance. He toed the party line. 'They are just friends – don't read anything more into that. My wife and I have met Emma once or twice. She is a lovely young lady,' he said.

Emma's relationship with the press was a strange one: they had started to probe into very private areas of her life – something that she disapproved of – yet she became oddly drawn to reading about herself. 'It became weirdly addictive,' she later confessed to *Vogue*. 'There's tons that's not very nice and I'm very, very self-critical, so it was like a drug to me. I focused on the negative stuff, so I stopped.'

An addiction to reading about herself in the tabloids clearly hadn't affected her studies, though. When Emma got her GCSE exam results, the grades she got were of Hermione-esque proportions. Emma got two A and eight A* grades. It was an amazing achievement for someone who had received such a disjointed education, in between school in Oxford and getting tutored lessons on set. Emma would later say that Daniel Radcliffe and Rupert Grint made endless fun of her because of her success. She ignored them. 'I'm so chuffed,' she told the *Scotsman* when she got the results. 'I'm over the moon.'

Meanwhile, the press reported that Emma was about to step away from the Potter franchise and go it alone in a film. Rupert Grint had been the first of the Potter kids to break out on his own and make a movie outside of Hogwarts. He'd featured in the 2002 film *Thunderpants*, about a boy whose uncontrollable flatulence is harnessed by scientists to assist in a space rescue. Daniel Radcliffe's first non-Potter outing was set to be a little more highbrow – after *Goblet of Fire*, he'd been cast in the Australian coming-of-age drama *December Boys*. It was revealed that Emma had been cast as adventurer Kate de Vries in a film adaptation of *Airborn*, a teen-oriented novel about airship pirates. Despite stories confidently predicting she'd signed on the dotted line, the film was never made. There are still hopes that production will eventually start on the film with a different actress in the role.

One film that was definitely being made was *Harry Potter and the Order of the Phoenix*. The fifth part of the franchise had a new director, David Yates, best known in Britain for his politically charged television dramas such as *State of Play*. Like others before him who'd come into the Potter world, he'd never read the books. 'Hadn't read a word,' he told the *Guardian*. 'It wasn't part of my world. The problem was I was dropping in on series five. So I went back and read all the novels and then I was hooked. I spent the next year working on the script.'

Emma now had to get used to her fourth director: 'It must have been really hard for him . . . All the cast and crew know each other and are buddy-buddy. Everyone is this big family. David wanted to really not forget the other films we've made. He wanted to take everything we'd learned and bring it all together in this one. He used flashbacks from the other films, which was so weird – there's a shot of me when I'm 11. Mike [Newell] and David are the first two British directors we've had, but they are such different personalities. Mike is very eccentric, very British, a very big character. And then there's David, who is very softly spoken, very thoughtful and perceptive – quite gentle. I had to adjust myself – it took a while for me to understand him, but now I'm really fond of him.'

One thing that Emma had to adjust to as filming began was the number of takes that Yates liked to get from his actors – 30 was apparently not an unusual number of times as Yates strove to get the performances he wanted. 'The word that I connect the most with David Yates . . . is truth,' Emma later told IGN Entertainment's news-and-reviews website. 'He always wants to find truth in all the characters and in each single performance. He had high standards but I think Dan, Rupert and I really relished that, as it stopped us getting complacent fifth time round. I think we all really learned something from him. It was really nice.'

The director was full of praise – albeit slightly guarded – for the young actress. 'I think Emma could have a great career,' Yates said. 'If she's smart enough to choose the right material, she could be fantastic. We have seen a fraction of what she's capable of yet.'

One scene where the performers didn't seem to mind the number of takes was Harry's first kiss with Hogwarts pupil Cho Chang, played by Scottish actress Katie Leung. 'We probably got it on the 30th take,' Daniel Radcliffe later said. 'My God, it was fun. We were awkward and nervous at first but, once we got it, it was fine.'

Yates would have to guide all the young actors – including Emma – through their first onscreen kisses. From the start he made sure the teenagers were made as comfortable and relaxed as possible on the set. 'The first thing I did was clear the floor,' director David Yates told film journalist Stuart Jeffries. 'Otherwise, the prop guys, everybody, turns up for a good look. I got Daniel and Katie to talk about their first kisses. You have to do that to make the atmosphere intimate. I told them about mine and they told me about theirs. It was about them getting lost in each other, to get them to forget they were on a film set.'

As ever, new actors joined the Potter family for the latest film. Oscar-nominated actress Imelda Staunton came on board as Dolores Umbridge, the pink and perky Defence

Against the Dark Arts professor who believes that naughty children should be punished.

'She's in a whole new league of bad guys' was Emma's evaluation of the new character. 'She's so horrible. There's something so sinister about her as well; it's a different kind of evil because she's so disguised. It makes it scarier. She's such a screwed-up, messed-up person.'

Giving Umbridge a run for her money was Bellatrix Lestrange, the unhinged witch loyal to Lord Voldemort, played by Helena Bonham Carter. Emma felt particularly drawn to Bonham Carter, not only because they were from similarly well-heeled backgrounds, but because film success had come early to both of them. 'She understands the pressures, having starred in *A Room with a View* when she was 18,' Emma told the *Sunday Times* in 2010. 'We're very similar. She needs to know absolutely every detail about each character she plays, so she asked me a hundred and one questions about Hermione and wrote it all down. Her script was covered in notes. I'm the same. I've read all the books several times. I have to know everything.'

Order of the Phoenix would be the only Potter not scripted by Steve Kloves, who claims he was asked to write the film on 'the wrong day' and turned down the job. It went instead to Michael Goldenberg, who'd previously worked on films such as the mystical sci-fi epic *Contact* and had been in the running to write the first Potter film before the job went to Kloves. 'It's a story about Harry reconnecting in general, and coming to appreciate what he's got, and at the centre of that, of course, is his friendship with Ron and Hermione, 'Goldenberg told the

Potter fansite *The Leaky Cauldron*. 'That's always been the core of the story, the three of them. There's something about those three characters, and those three actors, that's so powerful. And the performances that David has gotten, and that they've given, are just extraordinary. I really think people are going to be blown away. I really think it takes it to a whole different level.'

Emma was certainly pleased that the script put Hermione and Ron closer to the action. 'Ron and Hermione kind of took a bit of a backseat on the last one,' she said, 'watching Harry do all the tasks and stuff. So it felt really nice to kind of be back in the action again. I mean, nothing major. We had a couple of stunts to do, a couple of harnesses and that sort of thing, which was really fun.'

As ever, the production team whipped out their British road atlases to provide a diverse catalogue of locations for the film. This was by now an established sleight-of-hand trick used by producers in an attempt to avoid distracting the audience with too many scenes shot in one place. By constantly changing the back-drops, it stopped cinemagoers being distracted by spotting where a particular scene had been filmed. This time, locations included Burnham Beeches in Bucking-hamshire, Blenheim Palace in Oxfordshire, Fort William in the Scottish Highlands and a starring role for the Thames in central London for a dizzying broomstick flight down the river.

Back on set, Leavesden Studios would be the scene of a key moment in the development of the Potter 'kids' –

the first of them to reach the age of 18. Emma admitted that Rupert Grint's birthday made her very emotional – they really weren't kids any more. She bought him some surf-style T-shirts to mark the occasion and a party was held in the studio canteen. Emma, Rupert and Daniel had been through so much together; their relationship had changed and grown. 'They just keep me laughing really,' she told the *Daily Mail*. 'They don't tease me quite as much as they used to, which is nice. It's funny. It's been an intense and very long friendship. We've known each other for six years now, and have seen each other almost every day. I mean, they've seen me in every single state. They have seen me at my most glamorous and they have seen me at six in the morning with no makeup on. They do feel like my brothers. And we've been through all the ups and downs of this mad experience together.'

But for how much longer would they be truly going through the 'mad experience' together? As production on *Order of the Phoenix* continued, it was revealed that, while Radcliffe and Grint had signed on for the next film – *Harry Potter and the Half-Blood Prince* – Emma had not. Emma would later reveal that, during the making of *Order of the Phoenix*, she felt trapped by the punishing schedule that the film created. She experienced what she would later describe as a 'freak-out' about trying to juggle filming, impending A levels and being a teenage girl. 'I felt I'd been ripped into a million pieces,' she said.

Despite some press claims that the stumbling block was a financial one, Emma insisted that the issue was not money and that she'd do the films 'for nothing'. There were even reports that her parents disagreed about whether she should continue at all. Emma was torn over making a decision. 'I love to make people laugh and I love being creative, but there are so many other things I love doing too,' she later told *Entertainment Weekly*. 'I have such a structure when I'm working on Potter. I get told what time I get picked up. I get told what time I can eat, when I have time to go to the bathroom. Every single second of my day is not in my power.'

Producer David Heyman was typically diplomatic when asked about Emma's potential retirement from the franchise by the *Daily Mail*: 'It would be a hard thing to change and it would be disrupting. So, yes, I would love them all to see it through to the end. I adore them – I feel like an uncle or godfather – but ultimately they have to do what's right for them. This is their lives.'

Equally typically, Rupert Grint was a little less diplomatic: 'Emma doesn't want to do it any more,' he bluntly told the *News of the World*. 'She's tired of being known as "that girl from Harry Potter".'

What's more, Grint also blew a fairly large hole in the carefully maintained notion that he, Daniel and Emma were some kind of wizardly Three Musketeers, all for one and one for all. 'Daniel and I are distant from her now,' he was quoted as saying. 'We don't text or talk to her when we're not filming.'

Daniel Radcliffe was more tactful: 'It's fair to say that Emma and me have had our moments, but when you are with someone for six years, and you see them practically every day, there are bound to be moments when you just irritate each other.'

The public clearly liked holding on to the idea that the three young actors were constantly in each other's company, palling around off set as well as on. Emma herself would later admit that this just wasn't the case. 'To be honest, we see so much of each other when we're working that hanging out together would be overload,' she said.

A spokesman for Warner Brothers managed to hide his irritation when the film company was asked about the future of the Potter series. 'We're extremely confident that Emma will be back for films six and seven,' he said, a touch hopefully.

Emma clearly didn't share his confidence. 'I don't know yet,' she told the *Daily Mail* when asked about her plans. 'Every film is such a huge production, and it's a long time. Daniel and Rupert seem so sure. I love to perform, but there are so many things I love doing. Maybe that sounds ungrateful. I've been given such an amazing opportunity, but I'll just have to go with the flow.'

David Heyman almost seemed to be preparing for the worst when asked if he could keep the team together. 'In my dream world, we would have the same people for all seven,' he told the BBC. 'Whether that proves possible or not I don't know. I think the series is strong enough to survive changes – look at Dumbledore. There may come a point when one of the kids moves on. I think the strength of Harry Potter would survive that.'

Emma would later admit there was a divide between her,

Daniel and Rupert on this issue. 'Dan and Rupert have always been sure that they want to act,' she later told Radio 4's *Front Row* arts programme 'Both of them would do 20 Harry Potter films if they were there to do.'

Stories about the reasons behind Emma's non-signing began to swirl around the production, particularly as it was claimed there was a £2 million offer on the table for each subsequent film. 'The wait for me to sign the contract was much more about the fact that mine was a bit more complicated than Dan or Rupert's,' Emma later explained to journalists when *Order of the Phoenix* was completed. 'It just took a bit longer to work out in terms of scheduling and thinking about how I was going to do two more Harry Potter films as well as my AS and A levels and applying to university, because doing them alongside each other is no joke and you've really got to think it through.'

A deal was finally reached that reportedly involved her doing some filming in September, then taking a break to concentrate on her studies. She was also given every Monday morning off, again to prepare for her exams. If anyone had questioned how seriously she took her education, they were left in little doubt after negotiations were concluded: Emma had stood her ground – and won. 'We are thrilled and proud that Daniel, Rupert and Emma have chosen to complete the arc of their characters in the final two films' was the way Warner Brothers' Jeff Robinoy put it when it was announced that all three young performers would be on board right to the end of the Potter franchise. 'Through the years, we have watched them grow into extraordinary young adults, as well as remarkable actors. It would be inconceivable to imagine anyone else in the roles with which they have become so identified.'

'With Emma it was always, "Should I? Shouldn't I?"' observed producer David Heyman, when asked by the *Daily Telegraph* about the actress's apparent struggle to commit to the end of the series. 'She decided "Yes" each time, but it was, I suspect, a bit of a struggle for her. She wanted to cultivate a life beyond.'

Perhaps another reason for her hesitation was the unique way the Potter films were made. No film franchise had ever tried to pull such a young cast through a series of films over such a long period. What's more, Emma and the other stars were signing up to a series in which none of the Potter performers had any idea how their story arcs would resolve themselves – only J. K. Rowling knew. 'I don't know, there's this theory that she's going to die,' Emma told the IGN website when asked what she thought would become of Hermione Granger. 'I really want to see her putting her intellect and her just naturally very caring nature to some very worthy cause. So I kind of want to see her in another country protesting for the rights of house elves or continuing with SPEW – or just generally making the world a better place. Hopefully, she'll be married to Ron and have lots of beautiful babies. That's the plan anyway.'

Filming for *Order of the Phoenix* was completed and the deals were in place for *Harry Potter and the Half-Blood*

Prince and the final instalment, *Harry Potter and the Deathly Hallows*. It had been quite a year: as well as completing yet another film, Emma had taken on the might of Warner Brothers and bested them. She had also moved up several notches in the reach and level of her fame. Despite insisting that 'fame never interested' her, Emma had stepped into another more sophisticated social world and was by now taking part in a dizzying array of events, ideas and projects that reflected the increasingly broad brand of fame that she now enjoyed: she'd been asked to contribute to a special play put on in celebration of the Queen's 80th birthday called *The Queen's Handbag*; she'd been voted Britain's greatest female ambassador in a poll carried out by *Top of the Pops* magazine; she'd put her handprints, footprints and even wandprint into the pavement outside the famous Grauman's Chinese Theatre in Los Angeles; she'd become a fully fledged model, signed up by the Storm agency and had graced the front of *Tatler* and *Teen Vogue*, sporting top-of-the-range clothes by Yves Saint Laurent, Sonia Rykiel and Chanel; and the whisper on the catwalk was that Emma was also being lined up as the new 'face' of Chanel. She was everywhere.

Her fame was now beyond that of a mere teenage actress. But fame was starting to have its price. 'Yes, I do get stopped and sometimes it may be difficult to deal with,' she said. 'But I would much prefer to pay that price than not have any freedom. It's normally just tourists who shout "Hermione!" and chase after me. I have been in town with friends and been chased down the street and have had to hide in shops. Dixon's is my favourite hiding place. I shouldn't be telling you this because it won't be my hiding place any more, but I go and hide behind the computers because that's the last place they expect you to be.'

Emma's friends were now a small hard-core of Oxford teenagers. Many of her contemporaries found that being her friend was actually more trouble than it was worth. 'I'm not the girl they get the number 19 bus into town with to grab a coffee,' she told *Daily Telegraph*. 'I just get mobbed. It's an uncomfortable experience for everyone. Sometimes I miss the fact that I have never really been a teenager because I have been Hermione for such a long time.'

Around this time, she also found that the attitude of some of her fellow pupils at Headington School had changed too. 'It got harder as I got older,' Emma revealed. 'In the sixth form, there were a few girls who weren't nice to me, but I had a good group of friends who I was with all the way through.'

But hassle from fellow sixth-formers would seem relatively mild compared with what happened next. In March 2007, a man in his twenties entered the grounds of Headington School, looking for Emma. Gaining access to the school timetable, he found out where she would be attending lectures and calmly sat in on them. No one seemed to notice – probably because the man wasn't that much older than the students there – until he approached Emma after one of the open lessons and struck up a conversation. He started asking her a series of detailed questions about Harry Potter. Realising she didn't recognise him – and that it was a strange subject for a fellow student to raise – she alerted staff. The police were called, as were her parents, and the man was taken away. He was cautioned by the police and told to stay away from Emma and the school. She seemed to take the scare in her stride. 'The stalker stuff was exaggerated,' she later told *Tatler*. 'To be honest, my friends were more freaked out than I was. I'm quite used to it. My friends were quite shocked at how blasé I was about it.'

It's claimed that Emma was assigned personal protection to avoid a repeat of the incident, but she insisted that she had no plans to change the way she lived: 'I live a really normal life . . . apart from around the release of the film. I try not to use chauffeured cars and bodyguards and things like that. I take public transport. I like being with my friends, people my own age. My family keep me really grounded. I have a really strong supportive family around me and that makes such a big difference.'

Any unease that existed about Emma's safety at this time could not have been relieved by the steady stream of unusual gifts that the stranger end of the Potter fanbase began to send her. Bibles were their favoured gift. Emma had been receiving them from people who felt that the young actress was being led astray by the demonic nature of the films she was appearing in. 'Please don't send me any more bibles!' she said. 'I'm OK! I'm not crazy yet! I don't know how I can really top bibles because that's definitely the weirdest. I didn't keep them all. I just kept one or two.

I gave the others away. Actually a Japanese fan sent me plasters for my cuts that I had in the third film, which I thought was very sweet.'

When *Order of the Phoenix* was released in July 2006, it was a mixed bag of a film – out went Quidditch matches and set-piece action sequences and in came brooding resentment and teen angst. Harry is a disenfranchised youth, battling Dementors in graffiti-splattered subways as the Ministry of Magic starts to interfere in the running of Hogwarts. With defensive magic cancelled thanks to torturer-in-a-twinset Dolores Umbridge (Imelda Staunton), the teenage pupils band together to defend themselves against the Dark Lord on behalf of their beloved headmaster Dumbledore. '*Order of the Phoenix* is a real turning point for Hermione and her friends as they finally begin to take a stance and organise themselves,' Emma said on her website. 'I love the way Hermione develops in this film. She is the one who instigates Dumbledore's Army and she is so strong and fearless throughout even when finally battling with Bellatrix and the Death Eaters.'

Hermione's newfound role as a rule-breaking teen rebel creates shock among her friends. 'Who are you?' asks Ron. 'And what have you done with Hermione Granger?'

'Before, Hermione would rather die than be expelled,' Emma told the *Sydney Morning Herald*. 'It's nice to see she's come to a state in life where she's prepared to question authority.'

Perhaps the fact that Emma had a little family support

in the film helped her channel Hermione's newfound feistiness and strength. In one scene, Ron is seen chomping on some sausages. Sitting next to him is Emma's brother Alex Watson, who'd secured a bit part in the film. Alex – who years earlier would listen to Dad Chris read the Potter stories along with his sister – got the part after an invitation to visit the set from Emma. 'They [the books] captured my imagination,' Alex said. 'I got so excited that Emma said, "Come on set and see me at work."' As a result, the producers offered him the blink-and-you'll-miss-it role.

In the film, Hermione figures out a way to get rid of Dolores Umbridge, tricking her into the woods, where she is dragged away by an angry mob of centaurs. Hermione, like Emma Watson herself, proved that she can 'step up' with the best of them. 'I've been denying that I'm anything like her,' she told *Elle*. 'But I've come to terms with the fact that we're really quite similar. As the film goes on, the comparison is a big compliment. She stands for girl power, she won't let anyone mess her around; she's got two guys for best friends, but still holds her own. I love that she's intelligent and proud of that fact. She's determined, she never gives up, she's loyal, she stands up for her friends. I think she's kick-ass.'

Order of the Phoenix is topped and tailed by two great sequences – the broomstick flight down the Thames and a wand-off between Voldemort and Dumbledore – but Imelda Staunton walks off with the entire film with her demonically tittering, chintzy villainess Dolores Umbridge. Reviewers seemed to accept that *Order of the Phoenix* had a job to do in setting up the final instalments of the franchise and that at times the film – and the performances of its young stars – suffered as a result. 'The acting skills of Radcliffe, Rupert Grint and Emma Watson have improved,' said *The Times*, 'but not enough to truly flesh out the characters and provide the narrative depth that this transitional, plot-advancing film needs. They have got "angry" and "determined" down pat at this point, but struggle somewhat on the more nuanced grimaces.'

'The film has the look and feel of a contemporary horror thriller,' said *Entertainment Weekly*, 'particularly in scenes in which Harry has nightmares involving Voldemort. Also chilling is a sequence in which he and his friends battle the masked Death Eaters. These scenes, typified by sharp, fast cuts and terrifying visuals, suit the dark material. The special effects continue to be masterful, but villains are given a new twist, and *Order of the Phoenix* is all the more fun because of it.'

'Hermione and Ron are ever-present, but their significance in the story seems to shrink as Harry grows,' said the *Daily Telegraph*. 'But to dwell on a few weaknesses would be to neglect the obvious point – that Harry Potter is older, bigger and darker than ever. And no one would want to miss his journey. Yet the film is dark enough to engage adults, familiar enough to reassure us and fast-paced, as 766 pages are packed into two hours and 18 minutes.'

The *Guardian* also noted the slightly diminished role that Hermione played in the film, but still found space to refer to Emma as the 'thinking wizard's crumpet'.

But the reviews seemed to have little effect on the franchise's performance at the box office and the fifth film brought the Potter franchise to an astonishing tally: industry experts believe that the films had now earned $4.5 billion worldwide.

J. K. Rowling's final book, *Harry Potter and the Deathly Hallows*, was due out later that month. Emma said she queued up and bought a copy just like every other Potter fan. And, just like every other fan, she found out the fate of the three main characters in the Potter series – and particularly that of the character that had made her internationally famous. The teenage actress was where she was thanks to Hermione Granger – but the end was now in sight. 'It's quite hard to imagine my life without Harry Potter,' she told the *Sydney Morning Herald*. 'It's sort of hard to remember my life before. It's sort of completely taken over my life. I say that, but I've worked hard to make sure that hasn't happened. While obviously it's a huge part of me, it doesn't define me. I know who I am aside from this. But it feels strange that one day it will be over. In a way, though, I feel it will never be over . . . the books will always be loved and the films will come on every Christmas and it'll keep living on in kids' imaginations and adults' imagination for many years to come.'

And that, in a sense, was the problem. The end of the decade would signal the end of the Potter franchise. With typical Watson practicality, she had started to formulate her exit strategy. 'My biggest fear is getting stereotyped,' she told journalists at an *Order of the Phoenix* press conference.

'I want to do other things. One of the amazing things that have come out of this is that I have so many options. There's so many scripts and they are fantastic. I think I would like to do something different, maybe something smaller.'

Which is exactly what she did.

SEVEN

I FELT SICK

Emma was by now totally associated in the public mind with the part of Hermione Granger; far from getting annoyed about the situation, she completely understood it. 'Sometimes even I get muddled which one I am, because I know Hermione so very well,' she told journalist Lucy Cavendish, acknowledging the problem. 'My little brother Toby, who's three, gets very cross with me sometimes because when he sees me in Harry Potter he can't understand how I can be Emma and Hermione at the same time.'

The benchmark for how to shake off your Potteresque child-star image was set by Daniel Radcliffe at London's Gielgud Theatre in February 2007 in the play *Equus*. And Radcliffe set it *very* high. In the play, Radcliffe played teenager Alan Strang, put under the care of a psychiatrist (Harry's Uncle Vernon Dursley himself, Richard Griffiths) after he blinds six horses in a seemingly motiveless attack. The youth is a mass of sexual self-loathing, fascinated by horses to the point of an almost religious obsession. It's the job of the psychiatrist, Martin Dysart, to find out why the boy acted the way he did. The play was originally staged in 1973 and starred another child actor ready to make his way in adult roles, Peter Firth, who went on to star in the film of the play alongside Richard Burton as Dysart. He was well known at the time for the kids' TV show *Here Come the Double Deckers* – he's widely recognised now for the role of Harry in the TV show *Spooks*.

What grabbed the attention of the press and the public about Radcliffe's revival of the play is the section where his character is naked on stage. Radcliffe had psyched himself up for the role during filming for *Order of the Phoenix*, where he had to get over the embarrassment of his first onscreen kiss. 'I think the reason that it wasn't a problem or a worry in the slightest was that in the back of my mind I was thinking, I'll be naked on stage in six months, I've got to get over this,' he told Hollywood.com. 'Because if that's a worry then the whole nude-blinding-horses would be an even greater worry.'

A naked Harry Potter? Well, the tabloid headline writers had a field day, with variations on the theme of 'Harry's Wand' and 'Harry Botter'. Despite the sniggering, the show was such a critical success that it transferred to Broadway the following year; Radcliffe's gamble had well and truly paid off. Could Emma ever see herself being so bold?

'If I feel that nudity is essential to the story, I'll do it,' she told the *Sydney Morning Herald*. 'But I'm not going to be getting my kit off for something that I don't really believe in.'

Emma went to see the play to show support for Radcliffe, admitting that she, too, got 'a bit giggly and a bit embarrassed' about seeing her friend give his all for the play: 'I just sort of went, "You're mad, absolutely mad!" But when I went to see it I was blown away.'

J. K. Rowling also went to see the play. She told Radcliffe the play had given her a great idea. '"I'm going to write you naked in the seventh film now,"' Radcliffe recalled her saying. 'I said, "That's a joke!" And she did!'

Every journalist wanted to know if Emma was going to make such a bold move with her first non-Potter role. 'I won't be appearing naked on stage with a horse! But I am waiting for the right opportunity for me,' she said. 'Auditions are really hard and being rejected is always a bad experience. But I'll keep trying.'

At one second past midnight on 21 July 2007 – little more than ten years after *Philosopher's Stone* was published – the final book of the Harry Potter series went on sale. J. K. Rowling did a reading for 1,700 fans at London's Natural History Museum – and then signed 1,700 copies of *Harry Potter and the Deathly Hallows* for the audience. It took her nearly seven hours. The beginning of the end had begun. Those who had grown up with the stories now knew how the saga would end – and that included Emma Watson.

At the end of July, it was announced that Granada Productions were planning to make an adaptation of Noel

Streatfeild's 1936 novel *Ballet Shoes* to be broadcast on the BBC. It had previously been made into a six-part series in the 1970s, again on the BBC. Telling the story of three unwanted babies – dubbed the Fossil sisters – growing up in a bohemian but impoverished house in 1930s London, the book had been a favourite of slightly posh girls – just like Emma Watson – ever since. '*Ballet Shoes* has been loved by generations of readers, and is cherished throughout the world,' BBC Drama executive producer Patrick Spence said. 'The Fossil sisters don't just touch hearts, they steal them.'

It was announced that comedy writer Victoria Wood, Marc Warren from TV show *Hustle* and that man Richard Griffiths were to appear in the film, and that producers would be holding open auditions to cast the parts of the three Fossil sisters. Casting the part of Pauline Fossil – the young, beautiful drama queen of the trio – proved toughest of all. 'We saw every blonde actress in London, and not one of them was right,' said *Ballet Shoes* screenwriter Heidi Thomas, who'd just finished the BBC's *Cranford* series. 'It was like a nightmare. There were women in their twenties turning up in ankle socks.'

You have to feel sorry for the other young hopefuls who turned up to try out for the parts of Pauline, Petrova and Posy Fossil. Experienced young television actress Yasmin Paige got the part of the tomboyish Petrova; Lucy Boynton was Posy, the would-be ballerina. Boynton had made her feature-film debut the previous year in a Potter film of her own, playing the young Beatrix Potter in the Renée Zellweger movie *Miss Potter*. That left one sister to cast:

Pauline, the fame-hungry Fossil who's obsessed with auditions and becoming an actress. 'I was all set to go back to school after finishing Harry Potter but couldn't resist *Ballet Shoes*,' Emma told the *Daily Mail* when it was revealed that she had won the part. 'I really loved it; it felt so funny and real. It was also beautifully written. So much of what Pauline is experiencing is similar to what I went through when I auditioned for Harry Potter. She becomes famous sort of overnight and I could relate to that.'

As well as the parallels with her own life, the story was a Watson family favourite. '*Ballet Shoes* is such a treasured and loved novel by so many generations,' Emma told Screenvision, the cinema advertising company. 'It was actually my grandma's favourite book when she was growing up. She said to me, "You really have to do this project."'

There was one other reason Emma took the part: *Ballet Shoes* was one of Joanne Rowling's favourite books. 'Jo said, "You have to take the part, just for my sake,"' said Watson.

Screenwriter Heidi Thomas declared herself delighted with the performers who had been assembled: 'This is a captivating cast, worthy in every way of Streatfeild's gorgeous book. Emma Watson is a magical young actress. We are thrilled to have her on board.'

There was one other piece of Watson casting for *Ballet Shoes*: the young Pauline Fossil was played by two very young actresses, twins Nina and Lucy Watson, Emma's half-sisters. Casting was completed by July with Emilia Fox joining the line-up as the sisters' guardian Sylvia Brown and Dame Eileen Atkins as the imperious ballet tutor Madame Fidolia. Filming began in August. This was to be a tight turnaround as the feature-length TV film had been scheduled for Christmas 2007, barely four months away.

Emma essentially made *Ballet Shoes* in her school summer holidays. 'It was shot over four weeks – Potter movies go on for months,' she told the *Daily Telegraph*. 'I'm not classed as a child actor any more, so I don't work restricted hours. I was amazed at how hard it all was. I enjoyed it, though.'

The 400-year-old Ham House in Richmond-upon-Thames was a key location for the filming of *Ballet Shoes* – it was also used for the Spice Girls movie *Spice World*; girl-power fan Emma must have been delighted to share a setting with her former heroines.

The atmosphere on set was a very different experience for Emma: *Harry Potter* was all about the boys, but *Ballet Shoes* was an altogether more feminine affair. 'It was nice to be with lots of girls,' she said. 'It was a really nice change because usually on Potter I'm with guys all the time and I was with Lucy [Boynton] and Yasmin [Paige] and Emilia [Fox] and Victoria [Wood] every day. That was really nice – it was lovely. Obviously, we did it for the BBC. It was done in a TV format, so it was completely different to being on a massive big Hollywood blockbuster. We shot four scenes in one day and we were working six-day weeks. It was different.'

'Emma was perfect for Pauline,' said director Sandra Goldbacher. 'She has a piercing, delicate aura that makes you want to gaze and gaze at her. Our three young actors

Left: Emma with her dad Chris Watson, who she describes as 'up there on a pedestal'. © *Rex Features*

Below: 'My mum could be fearsome.' Emma with her mother Jacqueline Luesby.

© *Rex Features*

Above: A really good trio – Daniel Radcliffe, Rupert Grint and Emma in 2001.

© *Rex Features*

Below: At the premiere of the first *Potter* film with Rupert Grint, JK Rowling and Daniel Radcliffe.

© *Getty Images*

Left: Alfonso Cuarón, Emma's second *Harry Potter* director.

© *Rex Features*

Below: Mischa Barton presented the Orange Film of the Year Award to Emma and producer David Heyman for *Prisoner of Azkaban*.

© *PA Photos*

Emma with Katie Leung,
Robert Pattinson and
director Mike Newell
on the promotional trail
for *Harry Potter and
the Goblet of Fire*.
© PA Photos

Above: Emma's brother Alex.

Left: Emma caused consternation when she was spotted at the Burberry and *Vanity Fair* portraits party with indie rocker Johnny Borrell in 2008. © *PA Photos*

Above: With *The Tale of Despereaux* co-stars Dustin Hoffman and Matthew Broderick.

© Getty Images

Below left: At a party for Burberry in 2009.

© PA Photos

Below right: Emma with final *Potter* director David Yates.

© Rex Features

Left: Emma's 'wardrobe malfunction' at the 2009 premiere of *Half-Blood Prince* in London.

© Getty Images

Below: 'She wants to be a rock chick after ten years of *Harry Potter*.' With indie singer George Craig at the Glastonbury Festival in 2010.

© Getty Images

Right: Emma with JK Rowling and the haircut that caused a sensation.

© Rex Features

Below: Emma at a shoot for Lancôme in 2011 – the company described her as 'the icon of her generation'.

© Rex Features

brought such passion, spontaneity and realism to their characters. They were not afraid to let them have tantrums or narcissistic outbursts. I think they'll feel very believable to an audience today, and not like rarefied creatures with posh accents and perfect complexions. They are three young teenagers who squabble in their bedroom, but who happen to have extraordinary talents and dreams.'

Screenwriter Heidi Thomas also proclaimed herself a Watson fan. 'Emma's performance in *Ballet Shoes* is a revelation,' she told the BBC. 'She is maturing rapidly as a young woman and as an actress – her work is sensitive, subtle and intelligent. She is also incredibly hardworking. Our schedule was murderous, and she never once complained, even when she was white with exhaustion.'

Emma recalled, 'I loved making *Ballet Shoes*. It was so refreshing to work on a production outside of Harry Potter and a great learning experience. The days were long and everything seems to race along with such pace, but it was a very intimate production and I enjoyed every minute.'

Emilia Fox – whose parents were both actors – said she was impressed by Emma's application, especially in the face of such a stellar cast. 'Not having acting training added to her humility. She seemed very observant of the actors on set and showed a total commitment to playing Pauline's flaws as well as her charm,' she told *Vogue*. 'Unsurprisingly, she was thoroughly prepared and professional. But she was also immediately warm.'

But there was a degree of criticism levelled at Emma for appearing in *Ballet Shoes*. Some critics felt that accepting the part was an easy way out compared with the bold risk-taking that Daniel Radcliffe had demonstrated. But she still claimed she'd been so nervous on the first day of filming that she 'couldn't speak'.

The parallels between Emma and her character were uncanny. 'Pauline is headstrong,' Emma said. 'So in that way she's quite like Hermione, but she's not academic. In fact, she actually reminds me of myself as a child, much more than Hermione does. Pauline is utterly obsessed with being an actress and I was just like that when I was younger.'

Pauline 'does nothing but look in mirrors and recite', according to her nanny, played by Victoria Wood. She is obsessed about her forthcoming audition for an acting part and even has major concerns about signing a long-term film contract. 'I can relate to Pauline's ambition,' Emma told journalist Mark Warman. 'She'd sell her soul to be an actress. And I did always want to be an actress and I think I do still; but there's nothing reassuring about acting.'

Pauline's concerns about seeing herself onscreen for the first time particularly resonated with Emma. 'Tomorrow night, my face is going to be blown up as big as a house,' Pauline wails, 'and everyone will find me out!'

The line directly mirrored Emma's own feelings about stepping outside the Potter world for the first time. 'I actually really want to be an actress, a proper actress who makes it her career,' she told journalist Lucy Cavendish. 'I'm always expecting to be found out and I thought, If I'm no good, now is the time to find out.'

It made sense that *Ballet Shoes* was broadcast on Boxing Day – it's perfect holiday viewing while you're munching on turkey leftovers and that last remaining box of chocolates. Who wouldn't want to grow up with the feisty Fossil girls in the rambling London house they share with their guardian, nanny and lodgers: a sexy chain-smoking actress, a mysterious mechanic and a pair of retired academics? The film blasts you with period glamour and feel-good moments until you surrender to its charms. Although she is not high up the cast list in the opening credits, it's Emma's film. One stand-out scene has her exploding into tears as she caves in under the pressure of her character's selfishness. Crying, it appeared, was one of Emma's greatest acting skills. 'It's funny – I find it easier to cry than I do to laugh convincingly,' she told the *Chicago Tribune*. 'It's incredibly hard to pull off a laugh that feels natural take after take after take, that feels real. You can tell a fake laugh [snaps fingers] the minute you hear it, and that's something I really struggle with more than producing tears.'

Whether slamming doors in full-blown actressy hissy fits or sharing a bath with her fellow Fossil Petrova, the camera and the narrative linger on Watson. Emma told Alloy.com, 'One of the great things is that, in playing Pauline, I got to dress up and be much more girly. She's an actress, I got to dress up as Alice in Wonderland and there's a part in *A Midsummer Night's Dream*. Then she's in this film that's a period piece, so I got to wear a corset and an old dress and a wig. I got to have so much fun with all the 30s makeup. It was really good fun to do something that was out of school uniform and out of jeans and a T-shirt and something completely different. It was lovely.'

And the critics agreed. The *Observer* described the

production as 'Classic girl power'. It said, 'Boxing Day's new and visually sumptuous version was a highly enjoyable reprise of the tale of the Fossil foundlings, Pauline, Petrova and Posy, and their quest for fame and fortune, whose central message – "The world isn't kind to girls who can't support themselves" – is no less true now than it was in 1936, when the book was first published.'

'This is a beautifully staged production, hair and costumes perfect for the time period, as well as automobiles and household furnishings,' said the *Monsters and Critics* website. 'One of the treats among treats is hearing and watching Emma Watson as Pauline deliver a speech made by Puck in Shakespeare's *Midsummer Night's Dream*. She is perfection!'

The *Guardian* also approved – in a very *Guardian* sort of way: 'A proto-feminist, cockle-warming costume drama. Now there's a combination you don't see very often.'

For Emma, *Ballet Shoes* proved there was more to her than Hermione, Hogwarts and Harry Potter. She could exist outside the franchise bubble – she could act. 'I always had concerns that I was Hermione because I *looked* like a Hermione,' she told the *Daily Mail* in 2009. 'But what else did I bring? So this was the test. And it worked. *Ballet Shoes* was a small production, but it gave me the confidence to think I could actually have a career as an actress after the Harry Potter films. That I wouldn't just always be Hermione.'

Ballet Shoes came at a time of great change for Emma. She was looking to move away from Oxford to ease the commute to the Leavesden Studios and began looking at apartments close to where her dad Chris lived in north London. Brother Alex would also move to the area, leaving Oxford to live with Chris. She ended up with a rented apartment in Islington but the freedom would come at a cost.

'Since moving to London, I'm starting to feel the tension when I walk out of my door,' she told *Sky Movies* magazine. 'Harry Potter has such a high level of interest, anything – even if it's nothing – is news.'

Independence was beckoning. 'I'm learning to drive at the moment and I just can't wait for the feeling where you can just get in a car and go anywhere you want,' she told IGN. 'Just the freedom of that. I can't wait to go to uni or go and travel and just live on my own, have that first experience: cooking disasters, I'm sure, and not being able to do my own washing and everything. Yeah, I can't wait.'

Just how independent she could truly be was brought home to her shortly afterwards. Chris wanted to talk to his daughter. With her 18th birthday just months away, he had something to tell her. He sat her down and explained – in the calm measured manner you'd expect from someone with his legal background – just how seriously rich she really was. She claims she'd never really thought about how much money she had earned since getting the part of Hermione Granger. Now it was time to find out. It's believed the figure Chris Watson gave to Emma was in excess of £10 million. 'I want you to be able to understand that your money isn't some kind of abstract concept. I want you to have a feel for what it's worth and what you can do with it,' he told her.

To drive his point home, Watson sent his daughter on a three-day course in 'wealth management' at Coutts, often referred to as 'the Queen's bank' (you need half a million pounds just to open an account there). The 'assets and responsibility' course was designed for people between the ages of 17 and 23 – who just happen to find themselves with an extraordinary amount of money. The course used guest speakers to teach students how to follow the stock market and make low-risk investments. 'It's an important course because these young people are at an age where they're beginning to handle their own wealth,' a spokesperson for the bank said.

For years, Emma had essentially pretended that her money didn't exist – she was able to do this largely because she didn't really need it: she had her pocket money, she had a driver to take her to and from the studio, she flew around the world at the film company's expense and she went on skiing holidays with her family. Money – and how much of it she actually had – was a mystery to her. 'I had no idea,' she recalled in an interview with *Vogue* in 2010. 'I felt sick, very emotional. It was a real shock.'

The money and the freedom that it gave her seemed to create more problems than solutions for the teenager. Not only did the sheer volume of cash seem to baffle her, but Emma's attitude was: why would someone my age need this much money? 'The wealth side of it hasn't hit me yet because I have no need for money in my life,' she explained to *USA Today*. 'I still live at home. I eat meals with my family every night. I don't go out a huge amount. I don't really travel a lot. My life will not be motivated by money.

I will never do a film because they're going to pay me a certain amount of money. It's liberating. It means that I can hopefully make great choices.'

Emma insisted that, when she said that she didn't know what to do with the money, she was being deadly serious: 'I still haven't had all of my money transferred into my bank account. That would be stupid.'

After spending Christmas with her family – 'Christmas is a great time to just veg out and watch lots of really rubbish reality TV, eat lots of food and just catch up with people' – Emma passed her driving test in January 2008; she had her eye on a Toyota Prius. 'It's not the prettiest car on the road, but it's good for the environment. It's sensible and boring – like me.'

But Emma's 'sensible and boring' image was about to take a few knocks, thanks to her choice of male companions. First up was Johnny Borrell, lead singer of indie band Razorlight and former member – albeit briefly – of The Libertines with tabloid favourite Pete Doherty. Emma was spotted with the singer at a series of London parties spread over one eventful evening in February. The pair met at a party held by *Vanity Fair* editor Graydon Carter at the National Gallery to celebrate 100 years of photographs that had appeared in the fashion magazine. Along with Emma and Borrell, Lily Allen, Twiggy, Bryan Ferry, Will Young and Bob Geldof's daughter Pixie were also at the event. That most useful of journalistic sources, the 'onlooker', told the *Daily Mail*, 'Emma had gone over to speak to Pixie Geldof, who was chatting to Johnny at the time and Emma and Johnny immediately hit it off. It was clear they had loads to talk about even if they don't look like they have much in common.'

To the delight of photographers outside the event, Emma and Johnny then jumped into a taxi and headed for another event – another fashion party, this time held by fashion label PPQ at the Dolce nightclub in Soho. Emma, dressed in a strapless tan-coloured dress, and Borrell in his grey cardie did indeed seem an odd couple – but the snappers had their picture for the following day's papers. Two hours later, it was off to the Dorchester to a private party. Borrell was eventually thrown out of the hotel at 2.30am, when his behaviour got a bit too lively for the five-star hotel.

Borrell's racy reputation – he had boasted of his drug-taking past and declared himself a genius in the music press – sent gossip columnists into overdrive. The *Daily Mail* claimed that Chris and Jacqueline, Emma's parents, had told her, 'in no uncertain terms that she's not to see Johnny again'. That other newspaper regular, a 'source', said, 'They have always kept a strict eye on their daughter and are very protective parents. It was a huge shock to see their little girl coming out of a party with hellraiser Johnny on her arm. He's 10 years older than her and he's admitted to being a drug addict in the past. They're also concerned because his last girlfriend, [*Spider-Man* actress] Kirsten Dunst, ended up in rehab after splitting from him.'

Emma was so incensed by the reports that she was seeing the singer that she put a denial on her website. 'Oh my God, that is so not true!' she said in the online post. 'I only met [Borrell] once and we shared a taxi from an event to the after party, but never let truth get in the way of a good story and all that.'

The media seemed intent on getting Emma married off before her 18th birthday – preferably to either Daniel Radcliffe or Rupert Grint – but she was adamant that the single life was for her – for now. 'When I'm older I'd love to be married – success is meaningless without someone to love,' Emma told the *Mirror*. 'But he'll have to be intelligent, interesting and able to hold a conversation. Not someone who bores you out of your mind. There aren't a lot of gentlemen out there, unfortunately. But I'm waiting for my knight in shining armour. I'm sure he will come along at some point. Relationships are complicated enough without reading that you're breaking up or getting back together or cheating on one another every five minutes.'

And when they weren't trying to pair her off, the press were waiting for her to go 'off the rails' and kick back against her strait-laced image, and Borrell provided the perfect peg on which to hang the story they were desperate to write: Hermione Rebels. 'I do things in my own way, but I've never felt any need to rebel,' Emma told *Marie Claire*. 'To be honest, I've always had far too much freedom. I had a job when I was 10. I started living on my own when I was 17 or 18. I've earned my own money; I've travelled the world. What would I rebel against?'

She even threatened that her 'off the rails' years were ahead of her: 'I'm sure when I hit my thirties I will go crazy. I'll have this rush of hormones and madness.'

Emma was adamant she never saw Johnny Borrell again after that night, but it wasn't long before she was being linked to another man. This time, the event was the *Empire* Awards at the Grosvenor House Hotel on Park Lane just three weeks later. The ceremony was attended by Matt Damon, Ewan McGregor and James McAvoy – but it was events at the after-show party at Marble Arch's Carbon Club that really caught the columnists' eye. Emma was spotted getting up close and personal with a blond-haired man in his twenties. One onlooker said, 'He was definitely into Emma. As soon as she got there, they took a corner table at the back of the bar and were engrossed in conversation. They clearly wanted to be left alone. Soon after they sat down with friends, his hands were all over her and then they started to kiss.'

Perhaps mindful of the stir they had created, Emma and the 'mystery man' left separately and took different taxis away from the venue. One paper claimed that the pair met up later at a West End hotel. It didn't take long for the press to name the man as 25-year-old financier Jay Barrymore. It was the start of an 18-month cat-and-mouse game for the couple, with newspaper editors keen to grab pictures of when they appeared out together – or even when they didn't. They were snapped at art exhibitions, on the way back from the supermarket in north London or even poolside while holidaying in Jamaica – pictures of Emma were hot property, usually accompanied by some knowing quotes from mysterious 'pals' or 'insiders'. 'I try not to read it, but it's hard,' she told the *Daily Telegraph*. 'Who doesn't want to read about themselves? But it's always written with this tone – as if the person knows me. But they don't.'

For Barrymore – who was, after all, from the world of finance not show business – it was a hard task getting used to the attention. 'It's rubbish being my boyfriend,' Emma later admitted to the *Sunday Times*. 'People are constantly coming up to me, I'm always working, I'm always away – they don't get a huge amount out of it.'

Emma was about to learn just how far photographers were willing to go to get the picture they wanted in April, when she turned 18. The attitude of the press had changed towards her when she hit 16, but on her 18th *all* bets were off. Emma celebrated her birthday with a dinner at the American-styled Automat restaurant in Mayfair. Her brother Alex was there – 'About the only bloke I can go out with and not cause a stir,' she said – along with Potter co-stars Tom Felton and Katie Leung. Daniel Radcliffe and Rupert Grint were notable by the their absence. Emma finally made her way home at 4.30am ferried by Dad Chris under a mountain of presents.

Much was made of Emma's unsmiling, 'miserable' appearance – one paper referred to her as 'Her-Moany Granger', unable to fathom why a young woman who'd just come into a multimillion-pound fortune could look so glum. The reason didn't become apparent until a few weeks later. 'It was pretty tough turning 18,' she revealed to the *Daily Mail*. 'I realised that overnight I'd become fair game. I had a party in town and the pavements were just knee-deep with photographers trying to get a shot of me looking drunk, which wasn't going to happen. I don't have to drink to have a good time. The sickest part was when one photographer lay down on the floor to get a shot up my skirt. The night it was legal for them to do it, they did it. I woke up the next day and felt completely violated by it all. That's not something I want in my life. I just kept thinking that if it had happened a day earlier people would have sued their arses off.'

The so-called 'upskirt' pictures appeared in the press the next day – the *Sun* saved Emma's blushes by covering her modesty with a picture of Rupert Grint's grinning face. Emma would make a point of making sure she was never caught out the same way again. 'I find this whole thing about being 18 and everyone expecting me to be this object . . . I find the whole concept of being "sexy" embarrassing and confusing. If I do a photoshoot people desperately want to change me – dye my hair blonder, pluck my eyebrows, give me a fringe. Then there's the choice of clothes. I know everyone wants a picture of me in a miniskirt. But that's not me. I feel uncomfortable. I'd never go out in a miniskirt. It's nothing to do with protecting the Hermione image. I wouldn't do that. Personally, I don't actually think it's even that sexy. What's sexy about saying, "I'm here with my boobs out and a short skirt . . . have a look at everything I've got"? My idea of sexy is that less is more. The less you reveal, the more people can wonder.'

The actual day of her birthday was spent – like so many days in her young life – on set filming the next Potter instalment, *Half-Blood Prince*. 'Today I am 18. I can't actually believe it, it's so exciting,' she said in a video posted on her website. 'I just wanted to send you a message to say thank you so much for all of your birthday wishes.

I'm so touched that you're thinking of me. I'm having such a great day . . . I'm here in my dressing room at Leavesden, I've just had my breakfast [strawberries and Nutella – the spread was her favourite food] before I go down to set. I'm having such a good day.'

The cast and crew gave her a huge 18th-birthday card that they had all signed. On the back of the card were pictures of Emma and her young stars as they were on the very first film. She would later cite that day as being her favourite moment of making the forthcoming film. 'Turning 18 on set and having all my friends celebrate it with me!' she said.

That month, it looked like Emma's plans for an acting life outside of the Potter franchise were to get another boost. It was announced that she had signed up to star in a feature film – *Napoleon and Betsy*. The project had been bubbling under for several years with Scarlett Johansson in the role of Betsy Balcombe, a young noblewoman who falls in love with Napoleon Bonaparte while he is in exile on the island of St Helena. Johansson stepped aside when the part was 'skewed younger' – the polite way of saying that she was deemed too old – but she remained involved as a producer. 'It's a strong relationship but it's not sexual,' Emma told the *Daily Mail*. 'It's very complex. A touching of souls. She was a very young girl and he was this older, incredible man.'

But the project floundered – there was even talk of a rival project starring Al Pacino as Napoleon – and has yet to see the light of day.

'It's a project I love and am attached to,' Emma eventually said when it finally looked as if the film was not going to be made. 'I don't know if or when it will happen. I hope it does. I'm afraid that's the nature of filmmaking. You learn not to become too emotionally involved as scripts come and go and many of them never get off the ground.'

In August 2008, Emma got straight-A grades in her A level results in August. For a young woman with such an uneven education – her final coursework was couriered to the set at Leavesden from Headington School – it was an extraordinary result. A message was posted on her website to mark her success: 'We are absolutely delighted to let you all know that Emma received straight As in her three chosen subjects namely English literature, geography and art!! As you can imagine Emma is absolutely thrilled and we are all very proud of her.'

'I am very focused and very motivated,' she said when asked how she managed to combine the two so successfully. 'So I have tried very hard to combine being an actress with being a student, and so far it has worked out OK. I feel it's terribly important to continue with my education, in case acting doesn't work out for me.'

Potter producer David Heyman added his congratulations. He knew better than anyone how disruptive filming had been to her education. 'She's a seriously intelligent young lady,' she said. 'She got the highest grade in Britain in English in her A level. She's a fierce mind. In the beginning of the series she was less comfortable with being like Hermione. She was always really smart but when you're told when you're young that you're smart that's not cool. But now she realises that she's more like Hermione than she imagined and that's not such a bad thing at all.'

Her exam success had another effect: it planted the seeds of several interests that Emma would carry into adulthood. One was art. She would continue to draw and paint well after her exams had finished and loved to quiz actors such as Alan Rickman – who'd been to art school – about their shared passion. 'I guess I'm a little shy about my art,' she later told *Interview* magazine. 'But I love painting people and expressions and faces. I've always done art, though not a lot of people know it.'

Geography studies resulted in an interest in ethical trade – an interest that she would put into action in the coming 18 months. 'I had a very inspiring teacher called Mrs Bedford who taught me geography at A level,' she said. 'I did my coursework on the developing world, Fair Trade and different practices in the garment industry. I found it really shocking. People get so detached from what they eat and what they wear. No one sees. No one has any contact with how things are made before they put them on their bodies or put them in their mouths. I find it alarming that no one questions it.'

Emma was at a crossroads – and she began to question whether acting was really for her. She definitely wanted to go to university, but the question was where? Oxford ran in the family, but could she really get down to her studies in this country – and how would she juggle any film offers with her education? 'I'm at a strange age,' she admitted to

The Times. 'I'm not a woman yet, but I'm not a girl any more. [Film companies] say, "Oh, in a couple of years you'll be perfect for this." I'll be like, yeah, but I want to be studying English then, so it's going to be quite tough to choose between the two.'

Perhaps an Ivy League university in America would be the answer. This elite group of top universities – Brown, Columbia, Cornell, Dartmouth, Harvard, Pennsylvania, Princeton, and Yale – were among the best in the world and had been favoured by fellow performers in the past. 'Jodie Foster [Yale] did it, Natalie Portman [Harvard] did it,' Emma said. 'I think it's entirely possible to juggle university with filming.'

Meanwhile, despite confident predictions in the press, it turned out that Emma was not in fact going to be the new 'face' of Chanel's Coco Mademoiselle perfume, a job currently filled by actress Keira Knightly. The fashion house had expressed an interest in providing clothes for Emma to wear at premieres but a Chanel spokesperson said, 'Whilst we have a close friendship with Emma Watson, there is no contract.'

Once again, Emma used the Internet to put the record straight. 'Another media myth I'm afraid,' she said in a posting on her website. 'I love Chanel and have a fantastic relationship with [creative director] Karl Lagerfeld, but there has never been any discussion as to my becoming the face of Chanel.'

The 'loss' of the non-existent contract didn't stop Emma shooting into the list of the highest young earners in Britain, thanks to her 18th-birthday windfall. Speculation raged about how Emma would spend her newfound wealth. It turned out to be a mixture of the low-key and the extravagant. 'I got myself a laptop,' she told *Interview* magazine. 'I took my dad to Tuscany,' she recalls. 'He works so hard, my dad, so I rang up his secretary and asked when he was free, and I booked us a holiday. What else? Oh, I got myself a car. I got my licence last year and I love the Prius, even if my friends say it's ugly. They say I drive a brick.'

There would be one other significant present: a million-pound ski chalet in the fashionable resort of Méribel in France. 'That's a family thing,' she told *The Times* when asked about the property. 'We're all going up there for Christmas. I love skiing.'

'The house is Emma's way of celebrating her recent straight As at A level and finally getting her hands on some of her hard-earned cash,' a 'friend' told the *Daily Mail*. 'Like her co-stars, Emma has received some pretty sound advice about money. She always wanted a ski chalet and she's having a great time doing it up. She's looking forward to having friends to stay.'

Despite this, Emma still clung on to what normality she could, taking the train and the Tube when she was travelling to her parents' homes in London and Oxford and when visiting friends. 'I have a more normal life than people expect,' she said. 'When I take public transport, people are like, "That girl looks like the girl from Harry Potter, but it can't be her on the train." I get stopped by people, but that's fine. I'd never want to be so famous that I couldn't live a normal life to a certain extent. I can't imagine anything lonelier, just not being able to be part of the real world and being trapped and locked in hotel rooms and cars.'

But there was now no way she could still pretend that she wasn't seriously rich, as she had in the past. Emma Watson accepted her wealth as she had done her fame. 'Let's be honest,' she admitted to *Parade*, 'I have enough money never to have to work again, but I would never want that. Learning keeps me motivated.'

EIGHT

SEX, POTIONS AND ROCK'N'ROLL

Just as *Ballet Shoes* was about to be broadcast, Emma had started work on the next, and sixth, Harry Potter film, *Harry Potter and the Half-Blood Prince*. She believed that working on the BBC drama had helped her greatly – not only in terms of her acting, but also in deciding what she wanted to do with her life. 'Having an experience outside of Harry Potter really helped me,' she told the *Edmonton Sun*. 'I think it convinced me that this is where I am meant to be and this is what I'm meant to be doing – that I do want to be an actress. But I think I needed to have an experience outside of Harry Potter because, in a way, I was really plucked out of obscurity and given this role. I mean, I really wanted it, but it never felt like a decision that I made. It just happened to me. I felt that I won the lottery. So I've always kind of slightly questioned it.'

As ever, change was in the air and, after the brooding

angst of the last film, director David Yates was promising a change of direction. 'It's all about sex, drugs and rock'n'roll,' Yates told journalist Will Lawrence on the *Half-Blood Prince* set at Leavesden Studios. 'OK, maybe we should take the "drugs" out. Really, this film is more sex, potions and rock'n'roll; but there are all these wonderful things in our story. For a start, there's Felix Felicis, which is a drug that gives you perfect luck. You take it and everything goes right for you, but it also heightens your senses somewhat and you get quite "breezy" with it. Then there's a love potion that makes you very tactile with everybody.'

Emma was looking forward to some onscreen romcom moments with Rupert Grint: 'I think all of the stuff between Hermione and Ron will be really funny and quite fun to play as well. So I'm quite looking forward to all of that. I'm very excited that David Yates will be back for this one. I feel like *Order of the Phoenix* sets you up so well for *Half-Blood Prince* and it feels like there's unfinished business, that David Yates has more to give to the series.'

Hermione was required to throw some graceful wizarding shapes this time around, so an expert was called in to help Emma with her moves: 'We actually had a dance choreographer. All the spells had different choreographed specific movements that went with them and so we had a couple of classes like that, which was really good fun. And I think this is the first one that you really see kind of like the craft behind magic.'

Now that she had finished the books, J. K. Rowling found time for two on-set visits, much to Emma's delight.

'She has more input in the films now that she's stopped writing the books,' Emma said. 'But she's so busy. She's got a family and she's writing and everything. She's more involved now, which is really nice, and whenever I see her I get on really well with her. She's really funny – very, very witty.'

One of Rowling's visits formed part of the first read-through of the screenplay, where she sat next to producer David Heyman. 'It's always a very nerve-racking moment,' he said. 'You're thinking, Oh my God, what is she thinking? She made a note next to this one speech of Dumbledore's and we were walking out and she said, "You know Dumbledore's gay?" And I had no idea until that moment in time.'

The 'outing' of Hogwarts headmaster Albus Dumbledore became public during a question-and-answer session in New York while Rowling was on a promotional tour to promote the final book, *Harry Potter and the Deathly Hallows*. The Potter stories already had their enemies in those who felt they promoted Satanism; now they had another reason to boycott the books. Emma stepped up to defend the author and condemn those who used the news to attack the series. 'I couldn't believe what I was reading,' she told the *Sun*. 'This is the 21st century! I just could not believe the amount of fuss that was being made over Dumbledore being gay. I find it so shocking . . . Oh my goodness! I never actually thought about it before but, when she said it, I thought, "Oh, yeah, that makes sense."'

New sets were built at Leavesden for the film with an

astronomy tower being a highlight. There was also the usual sat-nav tour of British locations brought into play for filming: the Millennium Footbridge and Surbiton train station in London, the village of Lacock in Wiltshire (which has managed to preserve its 18th-century look) and Cape Wrath at the very far northwest tip of Scotland.

New cast members came on board, including Oscar-winning actor Jim Broadbent as Professor Horace Slughorn, who managed to make one of the more unusual Potter debuts. 'When this story begins my character, Professor Slughorn, is retired from his teaching post but he is being pursued by Death Eaters, so he is on the run,' Broadbent told the *Daily Telegraph*. 'They are after him quite seriously, so he has to change location and identity on a weekly basis, even if this means disguising himself as a chair, which, given his magic powers, is not a difficult thing to do. In fact, we first meet him as a chair. I have certainly been a lavatory seat – in a voiceover. But I think this is a first, the first armchair anyway.'

Broadbent – with a hundred screen credits to his name – experienced that slight feeling of intimidation common to many experienced actors on entering the Potter world. In an interview with the *Guardian*, the actor said, 'It was rather daunting turning up on set with all these young actors. It could so easily have been a nightmare, given that the five films have had such huge success. But the kids turned out to be terrific. There was no brattish behaviour or starry *Fame Academy* behaviour; they just get on with it.'

Producer David Heyman had a theory about why Emma

and the other young stars just got on with it: 'On the Harry Potter set, we have a lot of crew from the first film,' he explained to the Press Association. 'You can't get away with anything there, you get joshed and played with. You can't have any airs or graces. I've been very fortunate with the kids. There are so many cases of young kids being damaged by the experience or going off the rails and fortunately with Dan, Rupert and Emma that hasn't happened to them . . . yet! I don't think it's going to happen to them, they're pretty together, really good kids – well, young adults now.'

Director David Yates observed, 'Our cast are just getting that little bit older now and the hormones are starting to fly and for me it marks a real transition point between our cast as children and our cast as adults.'

There was to be a change to the usual pattern of release and promotion of the Potter films for Emma and all those involved. *Half-Blood Prince* had been scheduled for release in November 2008 – it now wasn't due in cinemas until summer 2009. Alan Horn, president of Warner Brothers, denied there was a problem with the production. He said the decision was made to guarantee the studio a major summer blockbuster in 2009 after filmmaking ground to a halt thanks to the 2007–08 strike by the Writers Guild of America. 'The picture is completely, absolutely, 100 per cent on schedule, on time,' he said. 'There were no delays. I've seen the movie. It is fabulous. We would have been perfectly able to have it out in November.'

In the end, another film filled the gap left by the shift in the Potter schedule: *Twilight*, starring former Hogwarts pupil Robert Pattinson, was released in November 2008 and it cleaned up at the box office, making Pattinson a worldwide star. 'I'm just gobsmacked by the level of excitement and hype around *Twilight*,' Emma later told MTV when 'R-Pattz' mania took hold. 'I'm very happy for Rob that it's been so successful. He is incredibly handsome! He is a very, very handsome man, so I'm not too surprised.'

It was also announced that the final Potter instalment, *Deathly Hallows*, was to be split into two films, which would entail a monster 54-week shoot. All three films would be directed by David Yates. The decision to divide the climax of the series into separate releases was as much of a surprise to Emma as it was to Potter fans – where in the story would the split be made? 'I don't know,' she replied when asked by MTV. 'I am as intrigued as you are. I am waiting at the moment to receive the script. It's a tough call. I'm sure it will be some cruel cliff hanger.'

'We've played around with a couple of places,' said producer David Heyman when asked by *Empire* magazine about where the split would be placed. 'And ultimately settled on a place that we think is very exciting, and I think quite bold, in that it's not necessarily where one might expect. You want to give a sense of completion, on one hand, but a sense that there's another piece, more to come.'

Cynics, of course, thought they knew the reason for splitting the final book: it would allow Warner Brothers to double their money. Among those cynics was Emma Watson: 'At first I thought, Oh my God, three more movies? I was overwhelmed. I thought, Is this a money spinner? I was very cynical and dubious about it. I was not immediately impressed. But I thought about it and talked it over with the producers and they said there's just no way we can fit everything into one movie. It will be too much. It won't be true to the book, we couldn't even call it *Deathly Hallows* because we might not be able to fit that story in. We'd have to call it something else, which would be crazy. As soon as I saw the logic behind it, it made perfect sense and I was totally behind it. But at first I had my reservations.'

'I swear to you it was born out of purely creative reasons,' David Heyman insisted to the *Los Angeles Times*. 'Unlike every other book, you cannot remove elements of this book. You can remove scenes of Ron playing Quidditch from the fifth book, and you can remove Hermione and SPEW and those subplots, but, with the seventh, that can't be done. I went to Jo [Rowling] and she was cool with it . . . and that was quite a relief.'

As a result of the new production schedule, Emma had some time to herself for the first time since she was nine. She planned to use it wisely. She went travelling and it was something of a novelty when she realised that she didn't have to worry about getting a suntan – something she was contractually obliged not to do if she had a Harry Potter film coming up. 'I've just come back from Kenya. It was amazing,' she said. 'I've just always really wanted to go there. I went to Masai Mara, and I went to beaches and it was a great place. I've just got back from Hong Kong too. I may go over to New York to see Daniel Radcliffe in *Equus* over there. I am going to make the most of my time off.'

And that's exactly what she did. With school finished, a freer Potter schedule and a gap year beckoning, Emma was able to cut loose, pursuing the things that she wanted to in the *way* she wanted to. First up, she caused a major stir attending London Fashion Week. Fashion writers were taking notice of what she was wearing and which designers she was checking out. '*Harry Potter* star Emma Watson was worlds away from her tomboy character Hermione Granger this week as she checked out the latest looks at London Fashion Week,' noted *Hello!* 'With not a strand of hair out of place and natural poise which would have made any catwalk queen proud, the 18-year-old actress more than held her own amongst the style set.'

'Emma Watson is making her way stylishly up the fashion ladder,' purred *Vogue*. 'Sitting front row at the Christopher Kane show yesterday afternoon, she really liked what she saw.'

Scottish born Kane – who'd already collaborated with celebs such as Kylie Minogue and Gossip singer Beth Ditto – had unveiled a chiffon and leather collection that season that had proved an instant hit with critics – and with Emma. 'I haven't worn his clothes before but I met him at a party and he showed me some of his dresses on other girls and I just knew I wanted to see more,' she said. 'I loved them. I've always been really interested in art and fashion. I've only ever been to one fashion show before – the Paris–Londres Chanel show – but this season I'm seeing this one, Giles Deacon tonight, and then I'm going to Paris to see Balenciaga, Chanel and McQueen. I really can't wait.'

True to her word, Emma headed for Paris taking in the French equivalent of London Fashion Week, viewing collections by Sonia Rykiel ('Amazing'), Chanel ('That was a big deal') and Giambattista Valli ('I don't even know where to begin'). 'I've been to fashion shows before, like the Chanel show that was in London in December,' she told Style.com. 'But this is the first time I've been to shows like this. This is my first time at [Paris] Fashion Week, and, let me tell you, it's pretty intense.'

As if to seal her fashionista credentials once and for all, Emma appeared in the September 2008 issue of *Vogue Italia* in a shoot with Mark Seliger, best known for his celebrity portraits for *Rolling Stone* magazine. The pictures saw Emma adopting a series of 'characters' led by Seliger's editorial style. One minute she was a Grace Kelly-style movie star dripping with jewellery, then a lovelorn princess by a lake and next a forest wild child.

'The Italian *Vogue* photoshoot was a fascinating experience,' she said. 'I was very excited to work with *Vogue* for the first time, but also to be given the chance to model couture. Each dress was so special and important and we only had a short time to shoot each one before it had to go elsewhere to be worn or shot by someone else. This meant the shoot had a real momentum. And the jewellery to match each dress came with its own security guards. I was terrified of ripping, getting mud, cake, a prop, or anything on the dresses! I felt like I was learning a whole new set of rules to a new game – just like shooting a film.

'Mark encouraged me to become a different person or

character for each photograph and so they all tell difference stories. So, in the end, I combined two loves: art/fashion and acting. I enjoyed the fact that Mark treated me like he would have done any other model and pushed to get the best out of me. I learned a lot and have found a whole new respect for the hard work models put into their work and for couture. A love affair has begun.'

Emma also enrolled in a course in Shakespeare at the Royal Academy of Dramatic Arts (RADA) in London. It can't have been easy for such a well-known actress to sign up for such a course, but it gave her the chance to brush off the slight feeling of inferiority about her acting skills that existed since her career began. 'I've kind of come from nowhere and gone straight in at the top,' she said when trying to explain the feeling of paranoia she had about her abilities. 'Where do I go from here? I feel like I need to backtrack and work my way through again. I'd be really interested to kind of train properly because I feel I shouldn't be here. I should have done so much more.'

While on the RADA course Emma was shown around the famed acting school by fellow student Roberto Agnillera from Italy. The pair became friendly and Emma invited him to a Cartier polo event at Windsor. The event was a good indication of the kind of high-end circles Emma was now moving in: Prince Charles, shoe designer Jimmy Choo, supermodel Agyness Deyn and DJ and producer Mark Ronson were all in attendance, along with a smattering of Rothschilds and Bransons. Emma was snapped with her arms around Roberto; a few days later, they were 'papped' again, leaving a bar in north London with Roberto lurking a few paces behind Emma carrying her shopping bags. As far as the newspapers were concerned, she had a new man in her life – or, as the headline writers would continually have it, she was 'casting her spell'. 'Every boy I'm pictured with is my "boyfriend",' she sighed in an interview with the *Sunday Times*. 'I'm never going to confirm or deny who I'm dating, but if they keep doing it the tally will get so high that I'll look slutty – not very Hermione.'

One thing the RADA sessions definitely did was open her eyes to where her future education might lie: thanks not to the course, but to her fellow students. 'Three-quarters of the students were from abroad, mainly the United States,' she told *Interview* magazine. 'I started talking to them about what they were doing at their schools, and I respected the approach. Here, I feel the specification is very narrow, whereas in America you're encouraged to be broad and choose many different subjects. For someone who has missed as much school as I have, I want to go back and discover what else there is. I always loved school – I was a proper, proper nerd. I just want that back again.'

The only way to find out more was to go and see for herself – to discover whether her feeling that an American college would be the best way forward was the right one. 'I'm really attracted by the liberal arts degree at US universities,' she said. 'They encourage you to study lots of different things so you do four different courses a term – so you can do 37 different courses in total – and choose your major in your third or fourth year. I can study so many different things which I find so appealing, whereas if I stay in England then I'd just have to choose one subject and study it for three years. I find that quite narrowing, so I'm really attracted by the courses that they offer in the US.'

Emma went to see as many of the Ivy League American universities as she could – and created a stir wherever she went. WATSON VISIT CAUSES UPROAR was the headline in the *Yale Daily News* when Emma went on a tour of the campus at the prestigious Connecticut university. Student John Song said that the 'Yalies' proved they weren't too cool for school when they spotted the actress in the canteen. 'Everyone just got out their phones and started calling people,' he said. 'There was kind of a little buzz around. Everyone was, like, "Oh my God, it's Emma Watson," but no one went up to her.'

Emma had lunch with some of the students and quizzed them about the campus, the courses and the facilities. It was student tour guide Drew Rowny's job to show Emma around. 'Emma Watson requesting a tour is a little bit different than Joe Six-Pack requesting a tour, but not so much,' he said. 'I think we treat everyone who asks for a tour pretty similarly. My sense is that she had a good visit, and that, who knows, hopefully, she's going to put an application in.'

She also visited Harvard in Massachusetts, where she looked at the accommodation, the admissions office and the impressive Annenberg Hall, said to bear a striking resemblance to the Great Hall of Hogwarts. 'I actually called my mom I was so distraught,' student Brian Hill told the *Harvard Crimson* after bumping into the actress as she did her tour. 'It was all I could think about for the entire morning.'

The visits seem to have generated more heat than light, as her pleas for campus tours to be kept low-key seemed to have fallen on deaf ears at some of the universities. 'I'm half wondering if that was a mistake,' she said, reflecting on her decision to do the tours. 'Because it just seems to have created more interest and more speculation, and now there are all these "authoritative sources" with different answers on what university I'm "definitely" going to.'

Tellingly, there was much less fuss about her visit to Brown University at Providence, Rhode Island. The independent coeducational college – its motto is 'In God We Hope' – prides itself on its campus made up of students from 50 countries, and part of the site dates back to its foundation in the 18th century. Officials at the university clearly took Emma's pleas for privacy to heart and her visit was well below the radar. Perhaps this was somewhere that she could study in peace.

Emma decided that it was the right place, but was clearly keen to protect the decision she'd made. Press reports confidently claimed she was going to Columbia University and had already registered under her middle name of Charlotte. Another rumour that she had accepted a place at Yale was quickly jumped on via her website. 'There have been several rumours spreading recently that Emma has accepted a place at Yale university after "telling fans via her Twitter account". We would like to inform you that Emma does not have a Twitter account [she would get one later] and that these rumours are false. Emma is still trying to decide whether she wants to attend university in the UK or the USA and hasn't accepted any placements.'

Despite the excitement her visits caused, Emma seemed to be coming round to the idea of leaving Britain for a university in the US. 'I never thought that I would want to go to America for university,' she told journalist Derek Blasberg. 'As a child, I aspired to go to Oxbridge, because that's where my parents went. When my dad talks about his time there, he says it was the most incredible experience.'

When she wasn't travelling the world, visiting universities, partying with the polo set or doing fashion shoots for *Vogue*, there was still the small matter of Emma's day job – as an actress. Her sole film credit for 2008 was a new venture for her, lending her crisp tones to an animated feature film, *The Tale of Despereaux*.

The film – the story of a jug-eared mouse and his quest to rescue a princess in distress, whose full title is *The Tale of Despereaux: Being the Story of a Mouse, a Princess, Some Soup and a Spool of Thread* – was based on an award-winning 2004 book by American author Kate DiCamillo.

The film had a fairly tortuous route to cinema screens. It was originally to be directed by Oscar-nominated French animator Sylvain Chomet before Mike Johnson was linked to the project. He was co-director of *Corpse Bride* with Tim Burton. Then Sam Fell (director of *Flushed Away*) and Rob Stevenhagen (an animator who'd worked on several movies, including *Who Framed Roger Rabbit?* and *Wallace and Gromit: The Curse of the Were-Rabbit*) came on board as co-directors.

Meanwhile, Emma was cast as Princess Pea. 'She's basically your quite generic princess,' she told Movies Online. 'She's very beautiful and she lives in the Land of Dor and everything's great. But then she loses her mother, and what makes it worse is that she not only loses her mother, she also loses her father because he goes into this state of grieving, and he just kind of locks himself away from his people and his responsibilities and also from his role as a father. So she's pretty lonely, she's pretty isolated, she's kind of literally locked up in this tower, and she can't really be part of the real world. So I thought it was interesting and felt very sad for her. I thought the conversations she had with Despereaux were really charming, and I really fell in love with the script and the book, more than the character.'

Emma was able to draw on her childhood love of Disney cartoons for her role as Princess Pea: remember that little girl who used to go to the shops dressed as a Disney princess? 'I loved *The Little Mermaid*,' she told *USA Today* when the film was released. 'I really loved *Pocahontas* – she's a free spirit, wild and bohemian. I'm a massive animated-film fan. And now I have my own.'

Co-director Sam Fell said he saw parallels between Emma and her character. 'She has this amazing celebrity around her and, like the princess, she's surrounded by it,' he told journalist Kevin Williamson. 'Yet, when we were working with her, we were saying, "Just be a normal girl, just be yourself." And that's sort of Pea's position in a weird way, where she's a celebrity but she just wants to have fun and chat with this mouse.'

Producer and screenwriter Gary Ross talked a good fight in describing the film in a documentary short that accompanied its DVD release: 'This is a brand-new classic fairytale, which may seem like a contradiction, but it really is. Kate [DiCamillo] chose to tell a brand-new fairytale but with a nod to what makes fairytales kinda classic. We're so lucky that we have a really wonderful cast. Dustin Hoffman, Emma Watson, Stanley Tucci, Kevin Kline, Sigourney Weaver, William H. Macy, Tracy Ullman and Matthew Broderick.'

Not that Emma had a great deal to do with the starry cast: with the exception of a few days in a studio in London with Broderick (as the mouse hero Despereaux), she worked alone. The pair worked on a key scene where Princess Pea and Despereaux meet for the first time. Her enjoyment of working with the American actor might have been heightened if she had known about his cartoon pedigree: he played Simba in one of her favourite childhood Disney cartoons, *The Lion King*. It wasn't until the film was released that Emma realised Broderick had been such a part of her younger years. 'No way! I didn't realise that!' she said when a reporter from MTV pointed out Broderick's animated past. 'I knew he was amazing anyway, but I didn't realise he did *The Lion King*. That is awesome. I have a whole newfound respect. I'm now even more in love with him.'

She didn't quite manage the same kind of bond with her other co-stars: the first time she met Weaver and Hoffman was at the premiere. The whole experience promised to be a new one. 'Honestly, I didn't really know what to expect,' she said. 'I read the script. They showed me some sketches of how Pea was going to look. I saw a couple of clips. Aside from that, I didn't know where they were taking it.'

But Emma threw herself into the role with her usual level of commitment: 'Working on Harry Potter and now *The Tale of Despereaux* . . . they are such loved books and popular characters you feel very responsible, you feel quite pressured to depict the character as they [readers] envisage it.'

On a performance level, she was used to acting with things that weren't there – years of performing 'alongside' CGI Potter creatures helped her with that. But this time round *everything* was imaginary. The best that producers could do was give her a toy Despereaux that she held while the recording sessions took place, for her to act and react to. 'To be honest, you feel like an idiot a lot of the time, particularly for my part, because it was quite physical,' she told the *Chicago Tribune*. 'I was being kidnapped, and I was being dragged around, and there was a rat in my room. There were moments you had to be out of breath. You have to kind of recreate this in a dark room, and you have to be quite imaginative about it all. So, when I'm screaming and being kidnapped, I was jogging on the spot for a couple of minutes beforehand trying to get me out of breath and get me in the moment.'

Emma recorded her sections over a long stretch of time, returning to make small changes and re-record passages of dialogue as and when the animators needed them. Her main concern was that she might sound too much like a certain Hogwarts schoolgirl. 'I guess I have paranoid moments where I will hear something in my own voice or I'll go, "Gosh, do I sound like Hermione then?" You know, I definitely have an awareness of it because I've played her for so long and she is so distinctive and she is so much a part of me. So, yes, I definitely have an awareness of it, but Pea was more gentle. I instantly felt a different person or character playing her. I definitely had a sense of that. I was worried about it but it worked out OK – I think.'

The Tale of Despereaux is a film that's easier to admire than like. With its painterly visuals, sweeping tracking shots and worthy but dry messages, it's the kind of animation that adults would like their children to enjoy, rather than a film that kids would clamour to see. There's not a single laugh to be had in the converging stories of a brave little mouse in a kingdom that lives for soup who 'loved honour and justice and always told the truth' and the characters his bravery affects: a grieving king, his doe-eyed daughter (Watson), a rat, a chef and a simple-minded maid. There are no songs, no hip pop-culture references and no gags aimed over the heads of children to keep the adults on their toes. It's like a meal that you eat because it's good for you rather than one you enjoy.

Emma's character of Princess Pea is said to be beautiful, like an angel. Her mother dies of shock when a rat falls into her soup on – of all days – Soup Day. There's no attempt at an accent or a different tone – what we hear is the clipped, upper-crust Watson voice we are accustomed to.

The princess becomes invisible to her father, who banishes soup and rats and the kingdom becomes a place of misery as the king is lost in his grief. Princess Pea finds herself in peril as she is held captive by the banished rodents in Ratworld. 'I felt really sorry for her,' Emma told *USA Today*. 'She says that, "One day, my prince will come," and it was really sweet that her prince came in the form of this goofy mouse with these enormous ears. I was genuinely interested to see how they [animated] it. I was always asking questions.'

As well as its stately pace, the story darts between the various characters before they are bundled together for the climax; one minute we are at sea, the next in a castle, then in Mouseworld, then with the rats, then a farm; then we go back round again. Like the soup the characters are so keen on, the story has too many ingredients. The title character doesn't appear until the film is well under way and the central message of forgiveness and saying sorry is delivered with the subtlety of a mallet. It certainly doesn't pander to the audience and is to be applauded for not trying to be hip and cool like many other contemporary animations.

For her part, Emma did her bit in talking up the film's positive aspects, as well as being grateful for the chance to do something different. 'I love animated films,' she said. 'So I feel like I can speak with a bit of knowledge. It felt really different to anything that I've ever seen before, because it felt like it wasn't patronising to children. The messages that are in the film feel really profound and philosophical, and I loved the ending, a serious ending about forgiveness. And my other favourite message was that every girl is a princess. I really love it. It works on lots and lots of different levels. I don't think it's just a children's film. I think anyone can go and see it and get something from it.'

The premiere of *The Tale of Despereaux* took place in Los Angeles in December 2008. Emma posed with an actor in a *Despereaux* costume with outsized ears and she planted a kiss on the character's nose for the benefit of the cameras. She was dressed in a striking navy-blue mesh-and-corset dress by British designer William Tempest, whose work she'd spotted at British Fashion Week. Tempest had already created a stir after designing clothes and accessories for Madonna. When photos of Emma's £2,300 dress appeared around the world, it created a rush of interest in his work. Commentators noted that she had never looked so sleek and 'grown-up'. 'She heard about me, as she came to my show last September,' Tempest told fashion journalist Rebekah Roy when asked about the Emma connection. 'It was a really fantastic opportunity making some pieces for her and she looked absolutely stunning in the outfit she wore. She has the confidence to pull it off!'

By now, of course, Emma was an old hand at answering the usual red-carpet questions – but this time around was something of a novelty: no questions about arriving on broomsticks, which magical talent she would most like to have or whether she had a crush on Daniel Radcliffe.

'It's really nice to be part of something different,' she said. 'It's nice to talk about something that isn't Harry Potter, actually.'

After the photos and the red-carpet interviews, Emma managed to meet up with two of her co-stars for the first time too. 'I had a real kind of weird reality-check moment,' she told reporters. 'I was in awe just today – sitting at a table with Matthew Broderick on my left, and Sigourney Weaver and Dustin Hoffman to my right. I was like, "This is insane. This is completely surreal. I have no idea how I got here. How am I really here?" It was mad. Completely mad. I've no idea [how I came] to be part of an unbelievable cast.'

At the premiere the cast sat down together to be interviewed by the press about the film. Sigourney Weaver – the film's narrator – was meeting Emma for the first time. It wasn't until that moment that Weaver realised who the nicely spoken English girl voicing the Princess was. 'We read all the Harry Potters out loud,' she said. 'And I didn't realise until I sat down next to you [addressing Emma] that you were Hermione. And we *worship* you!'

Despite its admirable computer-generated visuals and star-strewn cast – Potter veteran Robbie Coltrane also played a part – critics were divided on the charms of *The Tale of Despereaux*. Labelling the film as 'watery', the *Washington Post* said, 'It's a movie that simply has too much of everything, except a storytelling technique that grabs kids and makes them forget they have to go to the bathroom. It's a beautiful film, but, in the end, *Despereaux* is aesthetically charmed but dramatically inert. As usual with these animated epics, much depends on the vocal performances, and it's a mixed bag. None, however, provides enough buoyancy to get one past the structural sandbar that *Despereaux* erects between its audience and any reason to care.'

The *Daily Mail* said, 'If the story had contented itself with its main, heroic narrative, it could have become a massive hit. However, it over-complicates itself with no fewer than three other protagonists. On the other hand, the voice cast is spectacularly talented; the attempt to portray characters as neither good nor bad but fallible is a noble one; and the style and quality of animation is splendidly energetic and original, with nods to Northern European artists including Bosch and Brueghel. Visually, it's a triumph . . . It will probably underperform at the box office. To have succeeded, the film-makers should have concentrated on their loveable hero, and not tried to cram too much into 93 minutes.'

'*The Tale of Despereaux* looks like an illuminated manuscript brought to life,' said *Entertainment Weekly*. 'The screen glows with Renaissance golds, mice dressed like serfs, and a princess with Botticelli hair draped over a permanently foreshortened face. Too bad the story's such a mess.'

'The astonishingly starry voice cast is testament to the story's charm,' enthused *Empire*. 'While it meanders on its way to the requisite happy ending, the lush, stylised animation and courtly flourishes would win over anyone.'

Despite the mixed reviews, producer Gary Ross had nothing but praise for Emma. 'I think she is the most talented young actress of her generation. I think of everybody coming out of the Harry Potter movies, with all due respect to them, she's the one you go, "Oh my God, this is a classic movie star and will have a very, very long career." She has a Kate Hepburn or Grace Kelly countenance, in terms of her style and bearing and how articulate she is, and at the same time she is a hell of a good actress. She's somebody who has complete control over what she's doing and amazing facility. The girl's 18 years old. You're seeing someone who's going to be an enormous movie star.'

By the end of December – eleven days after the film's release – Universal Pictures reported that *The Tale of Despereaux* had grossed $35.7 million worldwide. It cost a mere $10 million. It was a hit, but in some interviews Emma seemed to be putting a brave face on it as the less-than-glowing reviews came in. 'When I read the script I knew it would be quite special and a bit different,' she told *This Morning*. 'It's funny, it's got adventure, it's got some good moral messages as well. I think it's quite bearable for adults to watch too.'

Although the film was a success, Emma again voiced concerns that perhaps acting wasn't for her and that, despite her considerable wealth, she felt insecure about her future. She seemed to see education as being a better option. 'The film industry is very unstable,' she said. 'Even if you're really big, you never know the next film that will be right for you. I think it can be very hard to have these intense times when [you're] making films and you're working, working, working, working, then it stops until the next thing comes along. It's nice to have something to fill the gap with and have that option.'

Whatever the choices she would make, *The Tale of Despereaux* meant that Emma had achieved one more of her childhood ambitions. This was of course the girl who wanted to be a queen, a fairy, a princess or an actress – or should we say 'mattress'. She was a pretty good actress; now she could lay claim to being a fairly reasonable princess too. 'I'm very lucky to play Princess Pea,' she said. 'How many people get to play a princess?'

NINE

ONE BEWITCHING COED

In the late nineties and early noughties, Britain's less salubrious youth could be identified by a particular type of plumage. From city-centre precinct to village green, it acted as a warning to others that it might be best if you were to give the park bench, playground or street corner that they were congregating at a wide berth. This flag of inconvenience was easily identified: a black, white and brown check incorporated into everything from baseball caps to handbags to jackets. It was commonly known as Burberry, though more likely it would be a cheap copy of the brand.

The distinctive check design had been hijacked by the chav culture associated with football hooligans and vulgar soap stars dressed top to toe in brown check. The 150-year-old brand needed someone who was a world away from the image described by one commentator as 'council-house chic' to front their new campaign.

For the best part of two years, stories had appeared linking Emma Watson to Chanel. In June 2009, it was announced that she was to be the new face of Burberry. The company's creative director Christopher Bailey told the *Evening Standard*, 'Having known and admired the lovely Emma Watson for quite some time, she was the obvious choice for this campaign. Emma has a classic beauty, a great character and a modern edge.'

The initial key photos for the campaign were taken on the banks of the Thames in London with a trench-coated Emma toting a £1,000 handbag and surrounded by a flotilla of young, pale and chiselled male models – Tom Guinness, Charlie France and Douglas Booth. 'I felt Emma would be strong enough to hold the campaign as the only girl,' said Bailey. 'And I loved the idea of her being surrounded by these young, cool British guys. Her charm, intellect and brilliant sense of fun made the whole shoot feel like a picnic on the Thames.'

The pictures were taken by Mario Testino, the Peruvian-born photographer known for his *Vogue* and *Vanity Fair* cover shoots and his portraits of Diana, Princess of Wales. Emma described working with Testino as the 'biggest ego boost of my life'. She saw the fashion shoots as an extension of her acting – and as a way of showing that there was more to her than Hermione. 'I've been trying to play different characters in each of the fashion shoots I've done and I hope that people can look at me differently,' she told the *Daily Telegraph*. 'It would be very naive of me not to be aware that it will be hard for audiences to separate us from these characters we are so identified with, so I think that has been my way of expressing myself.'

Burberry released a slick black-and-white video to accompany the shoot as a teaser for the 2009–10 campaign and there was a touch of mischief about the way it was put together – the music that was chosen to accompany the visuals was a Razorlight song, 'Wire to Wire', sung by Johnny Borrell, the man Emma had been linked with when she was 17.

The campaign was rolled out across the country – the high-profile nature of the adverts and billboards took many people by surprise. 'I was driving through Mayfair in London,' said Emma's co-star Robbie Coltrane. 'And there's the Burberry window and a huge picture of Emma looking incredibly glamorous in these coats and with the slight sneer that all the posh models have. The driver and I, who'd both been working on the films, said, "Christ, there's our Em!"'

As Coltrane discovered, it was hard to get away from Emma Watson that summer – she was everywhere. After the Burberry publicity, Emma reluctantly confirmed that she had finally chosen where to go to university. She had gone to great lengths to keep her choice a secret. 'I just want to keep it private for as long as I can,' she said. 'I probably sound like a paranoid nut, but I'm doing this because I want to be normal. I really want anonymity. I want to do it properly, like everyone else. As long as I don't walk in and see, like, Harry Potter posters everywhere, I'll be fine.'

Unfortunately, the carefully guarded secret was blown by

Harry Potter himself, as Daniel Radcliffe let the information slip in an interview with the *Guardian* at the beginning of July. 'She's incredibly academic, it's frightening,' he said, just about to put his foot squarely in it. 'Me and Rupert to all intents and purposes dropped out of school. And she's going to *Brown*.'

Thanks to Radcliffe's gaffe, Emma was forced into the position of having to confirm the information to the press. Ironically, she took great trouble to point out that she wasn't running away to the US to 'escape' from the media. 'I'm not trying to hide or anything like that,' she told *Paste* magazine. 'It sounds *so* geeky, but I really *do* like studying and reading, and, if I'm not working on Harry Potter, then my greatest relaxation is to sit with a book. That's how I escape stress – in literature. I always have several books on the go at any one moment, so it's no good asking, "What's on the bedside table at the moment, Emma?" because often I can't even see the table! I think that all that reading is just about the only similarity I have with Hermione, if you ask me. I'll be sorry to leave all my family and friends behind, but, hey, it's only a few hours' flight home.'

She was also clear that the move didn't signal the end of her acting career. 'There are end-of-term breaks where I could do something if someone asks me, and I liked the idea,' she reasoned. 'It all depends, doesn't it? Acting and studying are in no way mutually exclusive, are they? Going there [America] will mean a bit of "normality" for a while. It certainly doesn't mean that I will never act again, that's not true. There's been a lot of confusion in the media about that, and most of it is ill informed – I seem to have managed pretty well up to this point! But I do hope that it will be only a short time before I am known as "Emma Watson, the student from the UK" rather than "Emma Watson who starred in those Harry Potter films".'

The third section of the Watson Summer Tsunami of Headlines came just a matter of days later at the world premiere of *Half-Blood Prince* in London on 7 July – in atrocious weather conditions. 'We had the most amazing amount of rain,' Emma said. 'Unbelievable. And there were, like, hundreds of people out there, and they just stayed. They were drenched, drenched all the way through. And everyone stayed. In fact, it's probably one of the biggest crowds we've ever had. So, for them to have stayed, considering how awful it was, was just incredible. I think we have the most dedicated fans of any. It's amazing.'

A Burberry raincoat would have come in very handy in Leicester Square as the film was unveiled. Instead, Emma opted for a floaty and plunging vintage Ossie Clark dress from the 1970s as the heavens opened. Unfortunately, so did Emma's dress as a gust of wind momentarily blew it apart, exposing her underwear to the 3,000-strong crowd – and the waiting photographers. Describing it later as a 'small wardrobe malfunction', she added, 'At least I was wearing underwear.'

There was one rather more serious thing to notice about what Emma wore that night. She, like many of the cast, could be seen with a white ribbon on her wrist in memory of murdered actor Rob Knox. Knox, who was just 18, played Ravenclaw student Marcus Belby in the film. He'd been stabbed to death outside a bar in Sidcup, southeast

London, the previous May, just days after completing the film. 'We wanted to wear – as a mark of respect – a white ribbon, not only for his life but for other families who have experienced this traumatic crime,' said Bonnie Wright, the young actress playing Ginny Weasley.

Daniel Radcliffe said, 'I won't pretend I knew him incredibly well, or was his best friend on set, but I knew him and liked him, and what happened to him was obviously tragic and awful.'

Director David Yates added, 'With Harry Potter, you are surrounded by young people all day long who bring a great commitment to what they do, and Rob was no different. He came in and wanted to do brilliant work, he put his heart and soul into it, and you just think what a terrible waste.'

The film itself is believed to have been the first of the Potter series over which Warner Brothers put their foot down and asked for changes, claiming that the initial cut of the film looked too 'arty'. 'The only major run-in we've had since I came on board is regarding the look of this film,' David Yates told the *Observer*. 'We had a fairly major negotiation about its look. Bruno Delbonnel, who was also cinematographer on (French art-house comedy) *Amélie*, made it look very distinct and different from the previous Potters by using all these monochromatic washes. The studio wanted more colour added to it and we obliged. And actually it's no less artful with the new grade; it looks more beautiful, more inviting. When you're sending 28,000 prints around the world to goodness knows how many cultures, you need a show that pulls you in.'

Harry Potter and the Half-Blood Prince is indeed a 'show that pulls you in'. From its knowing opening shot of Harry being hounded by the press and paparazzi to Hermione, Ron and Harry planning their next step in Hogwarts' astronomy tower, there's a lot to take in. As well as action and thrills, the film has a job to do in laying the foundations for the forthcoming *Deathly Hallows* two-parter.

If more colour was added to the film in post-production, there must have been a very light hand on the fader. The film looks wet, grimy and postwar. Some scenes – such as the monstrous attack on Harry by a sea of undead creatures – look devoid of all colour. It asks a lot of the audience as it switches from horror to light comedy in a flicker. One minute Ron is mooning over girls, full of love potion, and the next he is near to death, fitting on the floor.

Of all the films, Rupert Grint comes out best here, as he becomes the target of a girl's affection (the brassy and bonkers Lavender Brown), while failing to see the young woman who truly loves him – Hermione. The situation – in Ron's words – gets Hermione's knickers in a twist. 'Hermione hates Lavender so much,' Emma told the *Mirror*. 'That she is with Ron would be reason enough, but I think Hermione mostly hates her because Lavender is the complete opposite of her. These characters usually face huge issues, like fighting evil, so it's easy to forget they're teenagers. For me, this film feels more like a romantic comedy than the others – we get to see them coping with first love, jealousy, insecurity and the usual things involved in dating.'

In one touching scene, Harry and Hermione share their respective heartaches, sitting at the foot of a flight of steps while holding hands – they are the best of friends and that's what best friends do. The way Hermione reacts to Harry came from inside Emma's family. 'I always pretend Harry is my younger brother Alex,' she later explained.

While all this is going on, Hermione is being pursued by the 'vile' Cormac McLaggen, Harry and Ron marvel at Hermione's really nice skin, Ron feels uncomfortable about Harry's attraction to his sister Ginny and everyone feels queasy about Draco Malfoy's transformation into a face-kicking, nose-breaking assassin. For Emma, the script meant a more human, vulnerable Hermione, as well as a tantalising reflection of her own personal experiences. 'She's so confident, she's always got the answers, but, when it comes to matters of the heart, she's left broken and a mess. I think that makes her relatable for other girls. I know I had such empathy for her. That feeling of longing? Longing for something, and it not quite being there? I know, a year or so before [we started filming], I had experienced things relatively similar.'

Producer David Heyman was promising a different side to Hermione in the new film, thanks to Emma's performance. 'I think one of the things you'll see in Six [*Half-Blood Prince*] is that she's really funny,' he said, 'as well as there being so much more depth to her pain – the pain that she feels about Ron and his inability to love her. Does he love her or doesn't he love her? She's amazing in this film – it's a whole move forward and she's aware of that.'

Meanwhile, Rupert Grint gets free rein to ham it up in a scene where he becomes an instant performance-enhanced Quidditch hero, after thinking he's taken a liquid luck potion. 'The Quidditch scene with Ron – I couldn't believe how funny it was, he just killed me,' Emma said. 'I couldn't stop laughing. Having said that, it wasn't my favourite to film – it was one of the coldest days of the year and we were out there for hours!'

Reviewers liked what they saw. 'What an odd situation the *Half-Blood Prince* creates,' said the *Daily Telegraph*. 'Four directors and six films into the series, it finally seems to have found its stride. It's as confident, muscular and comic as its predecessors were puny and timid. And, for the first time, it has a genuine emotional tug.'

Entertainment Weekly observed, 'They've found just the right balance of timeless spiritual profundity and contemporary teen specificity, of awe and humour, necessary to steer J. K. Rowling's enthralling seven-book saga to a satisfying conclusion. Will Hermione attract Ron Weasley? Will Ron kiss flouncy, pouncy Lavender Brown? Will Harry connect with Ron's no-longer-such-a-kid sister, Ginny? And will good triumph over evil? Stick around till Yates's final two-part Potter production, scheduled for 2010 and 2011, and find out.'

Showbiz bible *Variety* said, 'The film is clear-headed and clean-lined; now that he's at home with the material, Yates has made a Potter picture that is less desperate to please than any of its predecessors, itself a sign of series maturity. Emma Watson, perennially appealing as Hermione, has become a very attractive young woman.'

At a press conference after the film's premiere, much of the talk was of the final push towards the end of the Potter saga. 'We're working at the moment on *Deathly Hallows*, and I think we're all aware that this great juggernaut is reaching the end of its journey in a way,' said director David Yates, who was helming the Herculean task of shooting both of the final parts in quick succession. 'We finish shooting next spring and everybody comes to work with that knowledge in the back of their mind.'

Emma gave her feelings about the end of the series being nearly in sight: 'I think I will feel emotional about it in some ways because I spent more than half my life doing it, you know, and the crew is like a second family to me; so it will be very emotional. But in the same time, I'm excited because it frees my time to go do other projects. I'm ready to go and do something else now, it has been a while!'

A week after the film's release, a bizarre story hit the Internet and spread across the world within moments: 'Millions are in shock after Emma Watson died overnight in a car crash,' it read. 'The 19-year-old actress, most famous for her roles in the Harry Potter films, was killed while being driven back to hotel after a screening of her latest movie, *Harry Potter and the Half-Blood Prince*, when a car collided with her vehicle. Watson is reported to have died at the scene. Her relatives have so far refused to comment, only quoting that they are "too distraught" to speak with the media. Police are questioning witnesses about two men who reportedly fled the scene following the crash.'

A similar – equally bogus – story had circulated about *Hannah Montana* star Miley Cyrus several months earlier.

Emma's representatives were quick to release a statement of their own, in an attempt to stop the story in its tracks. It's thought the fake story was connected to an Internet virus. 'There is a very unpleasant hoax currently doing the rounds which reports that Emma has just been killed in a car accident in LA,' the statement said. 'Emma is of course alive and well and currently shooting the seventh Harry Potter film at Leavesden Studios in the UK. Needless to say, words cannot express our opinion as to people who make up this sort of horrid nonsense which is clearly purely aimed at mischief making.'

Online fakery involving Emma was at its height at this stage. She was clearly unhappy about it but at the same time she seemed to show a slightly old-fashioned view about having a presence on the Internet. 'I have got fakes on Facebook, Bebo, MySpace, the lot,' she said. 'And it's quite annoying. I can't understand why people put themselves on there. Some of the pictures that they put up of themselves make them vulnerable because anyone can see. I think the Internet is very scary.'

There would be more fake stories to come: Emma started at Brown amid claims in the gossip pages that she had arrived on campus on her very first day by helicopter. Of course, she hadn't: she'd arrived by car accompanied by her dad Chris. Despite this, the story spread like wildfire, with bloggers mocking her for blatantly not trying to fit in with student life. Unusually, a spokesman for Emma contacted the press to kill the tale: 'She arrived by car as did everyone else. She has not nor will at any time travel to university by helicopter.'

One thing that definitely did happen on the first day was that she was 'papped'. Snatched paparazzi pictures of her on campus, dressed in denim shorts and a white T-shirt, appeared in the press. She was on an orientation day with other students, taking part in activities to help students bond and find out what's on offer on campus. Some newspapers questioned the effectiveness of university security if a photographer could take pictures of Emma on campus. It didn't stop them printing the pictures of course. Mark Nickel, Brown's director of communications, said, 'We do whatever we need to do to ensure safety and privacy, and that applies pretty much to all students.'

It was a bad start to her new life. 'It was just awful,' she told *Vanity Fair* about her 'freshman' week, in an article headlined ONE BEWITCHING COED. 'I was like, "I must be mad. Why am I doing this?"'

Her exasperation was heightened when some fellow students approached her and asked for her autograph. On top of the fake stories and the paparazzi shots it was too much – she broke down in tears. Regaining her composure, she told the autograph hunters, 'I'm really sorry but I'm here to study and I just want to be a student. Would it be OK if I didn't sign, because you'll be seeing me around every day anyway?'

Emma has since said that that incident on the first day was the only problem she's had at Brown. Gradually, she got into the rhythm of university life; she even went to her first frat party and was shocked by what she saw. 'I felt like I'd walked into an American teen movie,' she said, describing scenes straight out of *American Pie* or *Animal*

House. Despite the parties all around her, Emma remained alcohol-free. Although she was old enough to drink in Britain, in America she was underage and felt that ignoring the over-21 rule would be disrespectful. 'Yes, I'm straight and boring,' she admitted to *Vogue* magazine. 'But I realised at a very young age that I was responsible for myself.'

'Being at Brown has totally taken me out of my comfort zone,' she told *Parade*. 'I'm so proud that I went to a different country to study and really spread my wings. My dad was very set on my staying in the UK and going to Cambridge. So my decision to go to university in America kind of came out of nowhere for my parents. It took a while for my dad to come round, but they both said they would support me if it was what I wanted. I didn't call home for three months. I'd send text messages, but it was too hard to pick up the phone: I'd just burst into tears. Dad told me, "Be yourself and you'll be fine." My mum was more like, "Make sure you wear a warm coat." She sent me thermals and English chocolates.'

She signed up for an acting lessons – 'I think actually I'm the worst in the class,' she said – and agreed to take part in a student production of Anton Chekhov's *The Three Sisters*. She had to audition twice before she got the part of Irina, the youngest of the sisters. 'I've no idea how we managed it – we didn't even have that long for rehearsal – but somehow we pulled it off – and got good reviews.'

She was experiencing a very new feeling. It took a while but she began to realise what this newfound sensation was: freedom. 'It feels wonderful,' she said. 'I have such a structure when I'm working on Potter. I get told what time I get picked up. I get told what time I can eat, when I have time to go to the bathroom. Every single second of my day is not in my power. Being at college, I took pleasure in the smallest things. Like, "I'm going to wake up at 10 o'clock if I want to." Or, "I'm going to eat a sandwich now." It was so liberating! I'd be smiling to myself, and friends would say, "Emma, what's wrong?" . . . and I'd say, "I don't know. I'm just . . . happy.'"

Inevitably, there were things that she missed about being so far from home: 'The food, the food! Marks & Spencer's food. I miss English chocolate. And I miss silly things like the adverts on TV.'

It was Emma's Englishness rather than her fame that caused a lot of the initial interest in her – some of her fellow students believed she put ten points on to her IQ every time she opened her mouth: 'At the very beginning they would pick up on everything I said,' she recalled. 'I'd say "jumper" and they'd go [adopts comedy English accent] "JAHM-PAH! After a while they just got used to it. My friend Madison made a list on her phone of all the different English slang I use. She has kind of like a translator so she can understand without having to ask me, "What on earth are you talking about when you say knackered?" Or what do I mean when I ask for Sellotape?'

Brown students seem to have gone out of their way to treat Emma just like everyone else, but sometimes – just sometimes – the temptation was just too much to resist. During one class when the lecturer asked the students a question, Emma's hand shot up in the time-honoured

Hermione Granger fashion. When Emma answered correctly, one classmate couldn't resist shouting out, 'Twenty points for Gryffindor!'

Of course, other commitments would constantly impinge on her university education; but, just as she had done with her A levels, Emma believed that by knuckling down she would succeed. 'I work really hard when I'm there and win my professors' trust that I *am* hardworking and that I'll come up with the goods somehow.'

Within a matter of weeks, she was back in Britain for a return visit to London Fashion Week. She was there as part of her Burberry contract as the show marked a bold move by the company to start shouting about its most iconic product, the brown check, which had been quietly sidelined during the company's rebranding.

'You know, it just felt like the right time for us,' Angela Ahrendts told Sky News. 'The city is celebrating 25 years of London fashion. It's been unbelievable the support we have had. We are thrilled to be back. A tremendous amount of business is done here. It is a halo for the brand.'

Despite attendees including Victoria Beckham, Gwyneth Paltrow and Samantha Cameron, all eyes were on Emma. 'Wearing a stunning metallic Burberry minidress and towering black heels, the 19-year-old actress turned heads as she arrived at the Burberry show,' gushed the *Daily Mail*. 'She even managed to upstage the perennially glamorous Victoria Beckham, who arrived in an understated black knee-length dress. Emma wore dark eye makeup and styled her hair in a loose up-do, proving she was perfectly at ease among the fashion know-how.

"Emma got the look just right," one eyewitness said. "It would have been a big mistake to try an over-the-top outfit. Her dress wowed the crowds but looked sophisticated at the same time."'

Burberry had chosen well in making Emma the face of their brand. 'She's a really hard worker, very ambitious but in a grounded, humble way, which is refreshing for the success she's had,' creative director Christopher Bailey told *Vogue*. 'There's no diva in that girl. I like the fact that she has a point of view. She'll jump right into a project and give it her all. And she's fun.'

Three weeks after London Fashion Week, financial commentators noted an upswing in Burberry's fortunes. Despite the recession, the company's sales figures for the second quarter of the year were up 5 per cent to £343 million. What's more, shares in the company had doubled in value during the year as a whole.

The Emma Effect was being felt elsewhere thanks to her 'day job', too. Earlier that month *Guinness World Records* named Emma the highest-grossing young actor of the decade. It was estimated that her star power had generated an average of nearly £549 million per film since the start of her career. She managed to pip Daniel Radcliffe at the post – he earned the studios a mere £537 million per film on average – thanks to the success of *The Tale of Despereaux*.

Back at Brown, Emma Watson found that she was fading into the background of university life. 'The amazing thing is that everyone here is interested in their own lives, so they aren't nosy about mine,' she told US journalist Jeanne Wolf.

'I'm used to people being intrusive and gossipy, but I can be anonymous. My best friend at Brown has never seen a Harry Potter movie or read the books. And one guy I dated didn't know anything about the films, much less that I was one of the stars, which I found hilarious.'

Emma ensured that her university experience was the same as everyone else's. Sharing a bathroom with seven others and going about her studies meant she generated less and less attention. One incident in particular brought home to her that she really was just another student: 'One morning I was walking down the corridor from the bathroom with just a towel and I thought . . . I must be mad, anyone could tweet up my towel. But no one did.

'I had serious issues with the code on my locker – remembering the numbers and how to turn it one way and then the other. I would be there for 15 minutes on the verge of tears because I couldn't open this bloody locker to get my mail!'

If Emma thought that she had finally achieved the privacy she had longed for, she was sadly mistaken. In November, the *New York Post* – under the headline HARRY POTTER STAR EMMA WATSON UNDER THE SPELL OF A NEW MAN? – printed pictures of Emma with fellow Brown student Rafael Cebrian, whom the paper described as a Spanish rock star. The pair were pictured at a New York Rangers ice hockey game at Madison Square Garden. 'They were sitting with Yves Saint Laurent creative director Stefano Pilati,' said an 'onlooker'. 'But Emma and Rafael looked like they were on a date. They were sitting very close together.'

Journalists soon found out more about the young Spaniard: he was a second-year student, a drummer with a band called The Monomes, and was a member of Brown's student-run theatre group called the Production Workshop. When Emma was pictured a matter of weeks later on a holiday break in Jamaica with Jay Barrymore with 'a face like thunder', the press did the calculation and decided that she was splitting from Jay to be with Rafael. As ever, an 'insider' was on hand to provide the lowdown: 'Emma and Jay, 28, were in trouble for months and with Emma at Brown University in America, the transatlantic gap proved too much for their relationship to survive. Emma has been spending a lot of time with Rafael and they are virtually inseparable.'

Emma maintained her silence, but in an interview with the *Sunday Times* in 2010 she set the record straight about her relationship with Rafael: 'He was never, never, never my boyfriend,' she said.

Despite this, Emma had successfully negotiated her first term – the start of a new life just as an old life was about to end. Despite the misgivings of her parents, the move to America had been a success. She had negotiated the tricky act of being low-key, while still being true to herself. 'I worry that I might be seen to be name-dropping or boasting, so I have to constantly be self-deprecating,' she said. 'I feel people are always ready to jump on me. If I show any signs of being a diva or ungrateful, they're just too ready to criticise. It's like they're desperate to find something they can hold on to. In the first semester I just didn't talk about my life at home at all. Now I've realised that's just stupid. Harry Potter has been such a big part of my life that if I don't mention it I'm being fake and my friends are only getting to know a very small part of me. Finally, I'm starting to be able to say, "Yes, I'm famous. Yes, I'm in the films. You're just going to have to deal with it." I'm not going to tiptoe around any more.'

Sadly, there was one incident that did put a damper on her university experience – but it didn't come about as a result of fellow Brown students. In October 2009, Emma travelled to Massachusetts to visited Harvard – one of the universities on her original list – to watch a Brown-versus-Harvard American football match. The student magazine the *Harvard Voice* got wind of Emma's visit and blogged that they would be 'live-tweetin' the game and possibly stalking Emma Watson, so keep your eyes peeled for that, too!'

As the game continued, so did the tweets. 'Let's go Hermione! Lolz,' read one. 'In enemy territory. Lookin for a certain witch,' said another and, 'WATSON FOUND. i repeat WATSON FOUND.'

Emma ended up leaving the game early, reportedly upset by the 'stalking' that occurred. She needed help from security guards to make her retreat. The *Harvard Voice* website later posted a picture of Emma, claiming their stalking mission had been a success and was initially bullish in the face of criticism of what they had done. 'There seems to be much ado about nothing over this photo and liveblog,' the *Voice* said. 'Understand that these live tweets were made to be intentionally outrageous and overblown.'

But in the face of severe criticism, *Voice* editor Alicia

Ramos had to release a sort-of apology to Emma – it was all 'a joke'. 'The presence of a luminary on campus inevitably creates much speculation and excitement, certainly without the help of an intentionally facetious liveblog,' she said. 'The *Voice* denies any efforts to "orchestrate" a mass mob of gawkers. In fact, the bloggers were never certain whether or not Watson was actually present and never once caught a glimpse of her. The blog was meant as an intentionally sensationalist parody for which no real action was taken. The *Voice* apologizes for any misunderstanding that the live blog may have caused and for any discomfort Miss Watson may have felt due to the post.'

Several weeks later, Emma was back in Britain after the first term had ended. She posted a video on her website. Despite what had happened, Emma seemed happy with life in America; the video also signalled the final chapter of the Harry Potter saga: 'I've just returned from Brown where I've had the most amazing first term and now I'm back filming over the Christmas Holidays. I've loved being in the States but it's so nice to be back at home with family and friends for Christmas. Wherever you are and whatever you are doing, I wish you a very Merry Christmas . . .'

TEN

WE WERE ALL
JUST A MESS

The mammoth shoot for both parts of *Harry Potter and the Deathly Hallows* had started in February 2009 and would continue until the early summer of 2010. Emma's involvement had been negotiated to work around her education. 'I had to beg,' she told *Vogue,* in case anyone thought that she had turned into a diva. The *Deathly Hallows* shoot was one of the few times that there would be any claims made that Emma's behaviour on set was anything but totally professional. The respected *Chicago Sun-Times* ran a story claiming that Emma had always been the most 'testy' of the young Potter stars and that this time around she was being 'more of a pain than usual'. A 'source' said, 'Daniel Radcliffe, Rupert Grint and the rest of the cast "are a dream to work with", but Emma is even more moody than usual . . . She's always complaining, showing up late and has upset both cast and crew members with her rudeness . . . She's really become a big diva . . . Everyone's sick of it.'

Perhaps the source of these claims would be traced back to the gruelling nature of the *Deathly Hallows* shoot. Compared with filming the other movies, the marathon schedule was a test for all concerned, particularly its young stars. Director David Yates pushed for truth and realism – and pushed hard. No matter how tired, wet or dirty Emma, Daniel and Rupert got, Yates wanted them to dig deep. Emma admitted that some days she was in tears. 'I was begging with him some days. He said, "It's so much better, you guys look so much more vulnerable. You are heroes but at the same time you're these bedraggled, unlikely heroes." It works, but there were days where I just wanted to kill him.'

'Filming the last two films back to back has been a very long schedule,' producer David Heyman admitted to the *Sunday Times* on the Leavesden Studios set, sounding almost guilty about what he had put Emma and the others through. 'I'm sure they feel jaded. It's true that Harry Potter has taken up half their lives. We've tried to do our best for them in terms of their pastoral care. We had a school set up here, but Emma was the only one to do A levels and go to university. Doing this must leave a taint, sure.'

Emma would later admit that the strangeness of life at Leavesden and the way her life had unfolded was actually one of the best aspects of her childhood. 'There's certainly been times where I've thought, This is weird . . . a *very* weird experience,' she told Radio 4's Mark Lawson in

2009. 'I'm very well aware that my childhood has not been normal or conventional in any way at all. But actually I like that. The three of us have been incredibly lucky with the people we've been surrounded by. They really have kept us sane and treated us like kids and not movie stars, which sometimes can happen, perhaps more in the States. We're not part of Hollywood. We grew up in Watford in an air hangar, and that keeps you pretty grounded.'

David Heyman agreed: 'The three of them are at their most relaxed here on set. Now they are so famous it is often easier for them to be here than anywhere else. Not coming here any more will, I'm sure, be like a bereavement in a way. Being so rich and famous makes them different from other people their age. They haven't had much of a normal life. It's hard for them to go out and they haven't been at school like most of their peer group. I'm sure it's sometimes hard, but they have managed brilliantly.'

The theme and feeling of 'bereavement' described by Heyman would occur again and again as the end of filming drew nearer with every working day. 'I feel like someone's dying,' Emma told London's *Evening Standard*. 'I know that sounds like an exaggeration but I really do. Everything is so linked to my life and growing up. But, at the same time, it will be exciting. It puts a pretty nice punctuation mark on my adolescence. I feel grown up now. None of us could say that we predicted this kind of love and recognition. It's just incredible. I'm just so unbelievably proud to have been part of this. I feel like the luckiest girl in the world.'

But she probably didn't feel quite so lucky while doing

some of the things required of her during the *Deathly Hallows* marathon. She would spend long periods wet – very, very wet. 'I hate to sound whiny, but it's horrible,' she told *SFX* magazine, describing the long days she spent filming the destruction of a Horcrux – an object created by dark magic that contains a piece of a wizard's soul. In this case, it was in water. 'This has definitely been the most intense, gruelling period of filmmaking I've ever done.'

One scene in particular – which ended up in *Deathly Hallows Part 2* – would be highlighted by Emma as the most difficult of her entire career: 'We get dropped by a dragon into the lake and I think it was January or February. The lake wasn't heated, and, because we had to get changed as part of the next scene, we couldn't wear anything underneath. I was lucky. I had my bottom half with some thermals on, but I was like, "This must be a joke." It was so cold. I think Rupert thought at one point that his heart had stopped beating. I hate being cold more than anything, so that was my most memorable day. I was like, "I can't wait for this to be over!" We spent pretty much the whole of *Part 2* soaking wet.'

There would be weeks spent running – very competitively – through Swinley Forest in Surrey as the film's lengthy chase sequences were put together. The three young stars raced each other as they were tracked by a camera attached to a zip wire to give a real sense of pace and threat. Director David Yates recalled, 'They ran like maniacs. Dan wants to run faster than Emma . . . Emma wants to run faster than Dan . . . And Rupert just wants to be anywhere just to keep up with the pair of them.'

Shooting the films so closely together was, Emma said, like being in the army. 'It's not very often that, in the middle of the filmmaking process, you stop yourself and go, "This is going to be awesome" and I've done that on a number of occasions,' she told the ComingSoon movie website. 'We've done this amazing scene in the forest where we're getting chased by the Snatchers, and I've never done anything like it, nothing even close. I've never really done any serious stunts or any real action, and it's so exciting and just really dynamic. Because all of us are now finished with school and we're all just totally focused on this finale. It's out of Hogwarts, it's just about the three of us. It's going to be . . . well, I hope it's going to be brilliant and it feels totally different. I feel like I'm on a different film.'

Then there were long, improvised sequences as Hermione is tortured by Death Eater Bellatrix Lestrange, played with typical mad goth enthusiasm by Helena Bonham Carter. Emma, keen to make the scenes as realistic possible, asked production staff to source some documentaries where real-life victims of torture described how they felt while the terrible act was being carried out. 'It was quite horrible to do, but it was a real challenge. I think as Bellatrix, she [Bonham Carter] is just terrifying because she looks so unhinged, she looks so crazy. I don't think she actually enjoyed doing it. I guess it showed that I was doing a good job that she felt uncomfortable.'

Director David Yates would leave his camera running for up to five minutes as Emma and Bonham Carter tried different ways of building up the tension between their characters, as Bellatrix tries to find out how the trio managed to get their hands on the Gryffindor sword. 'Emma wanted to do research, she was really keen to get it right,' said David Yates. 'The first time we did it, I yell, "Cut!" Emma said, "You cut too early! You cut too early!" She was getting to this intense point. And I said, "Well, it was getting scary, Ems!" And she said, "No, no, no, no, let me try, let me try." There were one or two moments that were really powerful, where Emma was able to just let go a little bit and forget for a moment that she was acting. And the screams were quite horrible to listen to. It was a very odd energy in the room. She was kind of exploring and exorcising demons really, and serving the scene doing that.'

There was one other strange element to put in the mix during the filming of the sequence – the reaction that the sight of one striking-looking woman torturing another had on male onlookers. 'It was really funny because Helena and I were very much [saying] this is going to be terrifying, were planning how to make it as horrible as possible,' Emma said. 'And most of the blokes on set were just being a bit pervy about it to be honest. Very unprofessional. We were very unimpressed.'

Emma later described the sequences as 'the weirdest thing ever. It was like having an out-of-body experience. It's the most intense thing I've ever done. It felt like an eternity. It felt like forever.'

The significance was not lost on David Yates: 'I felt in that moment, and in that day and in that room, she kind of crossed the line as an actress. She discovered something within herself that will make her a great actor.'

Emma was full of praise for the director: 'He was very good. He's very calm, which is great for me, because there are days when I just panicked, I mean really just . . . "David, I don't know how to do this!" I didn't know how to *act* . . . I've never been tortured before, I have no idea how to pull that off. There was some really hard stuff to do, like what it's like to erase your parents' memories and walk out the door. I think for me, I have quite an academic, like a "heady" approach, I guess, to the way that I act, and us just talking through what it meant, what does it mean for her? How does it relate to her past? What does she think about this? Having the time to be very clear in my head about what exactly everything was allowed me to give a really good performance. He's very patient, which is so nice. I never felt like I was being hurried, so that was nice. He's very good like that, he's very gentle.'

There would be other moments of on-set torture for Emma too. They would involve the two actors she had known since they were all children, Daniel Radcliffe and Rupert Grint. She would have to deliver an onscreen kiss. Not with one of them, but with both of them. 'I have to think myself back a couple of years, because Hermione's never had a boyfriend, never been kissed by a boy,' Emma reasoned.

But the more she thought about it, the more the prospect began to loom large in the shooting schedule. It would be 'like incest', she said. 'I had to kiss what feels like my two brothers – I mean, that was pretty bad,' she told the Scholastic website. 'I would definitely count that as an embarrassing, awkward moment. Neither of them were bad kissers – that's not the point – but it definitely was pretty awkward.'

First up were Emma and Rupert – the pair steeled themselves for the awkward moment they knew was coming. 'Kissing Rupert's going to be *sooo* awkward,' Emma told the *Mail on Sunday*. 'I'm trying not to think about it . . . it's all part of the job I guess. Don't tell him I said that. Rupert's lovely. Girls would probably give their left arm to be in my position, so I'm certainly not complaining.'

The two young actors agreed to make the best of it and get it done as quickly as possible. They also both agreed to brush their teeth beforehand. Emma revealed, 'I was like, "Do I use tongue? Do I not use tongue? Do I cover my teeth? What do I do? Do I go first?" Oh my God!'

The scene took six takes. 'We were determined to get it right the first time,' said Grint. 'But our first try was a disaster because we both felt so self-conscious and we couldn't stop laughing.'

The laughter wasn't the only thing that was a touch infectious when the scene was filmed: so was Rupert Grint. 'It was quite scary when they first told me I had swine flu,' he explained to the *Daily Telegraph*. 'After what's been in the press and stuff, I thought, Am I going to die? But it was just like any other flu I've had before. I just had a sore throat,' he said.

Journalists had been asking Emma about 'The Kiss' since the *Deathly Hallows* book was first published in the summer of 2007. Though she understood there was a lot riding on the scene, she took the opportunity when asked about it to take a gentle but well-aimed potshot at another film series that was currently filling cinemas. 'I suppose I understand. This kiss between Ron and Hermione is highly anticipated, it's been building up for eight films now,' she explained to *Empire* magazine. 'And Harry Potter . . . it's not *Twilight*, you know. We're not selling sex. So, whenever there is a hint of that, everybody gets terribly excited. In fact, it was horribly awkward; we couldn't stop laughing. The nicest thing about it was, before we did it, we turned to each other and were like, "God, this is going to be awful, isn't it?" But hopefully it will look good.'

When it came to kissing Daniel – 'I'd already kissed Rupert . . . at that point I was in my stride' – there would be an added awkwardness: they'd both be half-naked and covered in silver paint. 'It was the weirdest thing ever,' Emma said. 'And they only told us about the silver body paint the day before. They were like, "Oh, and, PS, we hope you don't mind but we'd like you both to be topless and covered in silver paint." I was like, "Oookay," if it wasn't weird enough before. So, yeah, it was bizarre. Luckily, Dan is very funny and talkative and we could just have a laugh about it. Kissing Rupert, he's slightly more quiet so I was like, "Oh, God, what's he thinking?" Whereas the whole time with Dan I knew *exactly* what he was thinking, so that helped.'

The scene – a vision designed to put doubt into the mind of Ron about what was going on behind his back – was described as 'very sexy and very intriguing' by director David Yates. Daniel Radcliffe was certainly intrigued at how intensely Emma 'attacked' the scene. 'I always thought it was going to be this soft sensual sort of moment, and suddenly there was this vigorous kissing happening to me,' Radcliffe told ITV1's *Daybreak* programme. 'She is a bit of an animal . . . But then, I'm not complaining. There are tens of thousands of men that would cut off limbs to be in that position. Rupert actually had to leave the set, because he was laughing that much.'

'Dan's been telling people I pounced on him and that I'm an animal,' Emma responded. 'I just wanted to make it as real as possible. It obviously had to be something that would disturb Ron and make him really jealous, so from Hermione's end it had to be passionate. It's written all over Rupert's face that he really loves her.'

Daniel continued, 'It was kind of weird. It's a bit like kissing your sister. I'm not complaining! It was good. It was *vigorous*. For me, I wasn't too freaked out. But it's a bigger deal for Emma. I think it generally is a bigger deal for girls.'

'It is full-on,' Emma told MTV News. 'Actually, I forgot how full-on it was until I saw the movie, and I was like, "Blimey, where did that come from?"'

Emma and Daniel had another tender scene to perform. Director David Yates would later tell the *Daily Mail* that it was his favourite moment. 'It's where Hermione and Harry dance together and is not in the book,' he said. 'It's something we create for the film and is actually very tender. They also reveal some secrets about each other while dancing.'

'Me and Hermione just start dancing to this song – together,' Daniel told ITV1. 'It's a slow song and a slow dance. It is a very lovely and tender scene and it's the only moment between Harry and Hermione where you go, "Are they about to do something?"'

A mixture of the story's intensity, the sheer length of the shoot and the fact that Emma was jetting back and forth to maintain her courses at Brown took its toll: 'There were days where it was so unglamorous. There were days where I'd fall asleep anywhere – our on-set photographer has pictures of me falling asleep in chairs, on the floor, in the middle of the set. Curled up. Like a cat.'

Along with the running, being continually dropped into water, the torture and being made to kiss young men who were like her brothers, there was at least one moment of glamour for Emma to savour. During the filming of Bill Weasley and Fleur Delacour's wedding, Emma finally got to dress up. 'I get to wear a pretty spectacular outfit. It's kind of sexy, actually . . . by Hermione standards. It's red, quite low-cut . . . She's a young woman now so she's allowed to be a bit sexy.'

Finally, there was the issue of how to film the ending of the entire series, where we see the older versions of Harry, Ron, Ginny and Hermione and discover how their lives have turned out in middle age. Various methods were tried to create the effect, including some long stints in the makeup chair. 'It was a pretty lengthy process,' she told the Scholastic website. 'I think it was, like, over two hours. But it was really subtle. They had this thin film that they put on our faces which went into our wrinkles to make all of that happen. Really subtle details made a huge difference. I wore fake teeth and a wig, but it all looked really real, so it was cool.'

Despite the relatively light touch of the makeup department, Emma vowed that she did not want to undergo the experience again: 'Prosthetics are horrible. I'm going to avoid doing a movie with prosthetics, like my life depends on it. I'm glad I had a taste of that experience, enough to know it's miserable.'

Instead of makeup, producer David Heyman had been keen to use the digital technology used to enable Brad Pitt to age more than 60 years backwards from looking like a very old man in *The Curious Case of Benjamin Button*. 'I am nervous about that,' Daniel Radcliffe told *Empire*, 'because, if it's good I'll be really, really pleased; if it's not good and that's what people are left with, that would be awful. If it's a choice between having me, Rupert and Emma looking a bit stupid and it being slightly comical or having other actors play us, I would go for other actors every time. So, we'll see.'

Director David Yates felt there was a great deal at stake for Emma and her co-stars this time around, and *Deathly Hallows* was their chance to show what they were made of. 'They're getting older,' he told the Collider film website. 'Which just means they've got more resources at their fingertips because, as an actor, everything you do comes from your experience of life – more than your experience on a film set, frankly, sometimes. It's the last time they're ever going to play these characters. They had a stake here to prove themselves to the fan base and to a global audience. The material's a bit richer and more nuanced this time. A bit more melancholic. They get more time with these quite grown-up scenes and I always push them to try to find authenticity in what they do together. That's what I want from them. So all those things together meant, I think, that they're able to give more than they've ever had a chance to give before and they were so excited when they first read the script. I sat with them in the boardroom at Leavesden, and we sat and they read it and they were so buzzed because they got to do all these things together, which was less about magic and more about them.'

There were some final additions to the stellar list of British acting talent that had leant weight to the Potter films throughout the series. Rhys Ifans appeared as Xenophilius Lovegood, father of Luna and editor of the wizarding magazine *The Quibbler*. 'When you're a British actor and you get the call from Harry Potter, that's like getting your stripes,' he said about getting the part. 'It was great. You end up on set and there's all these actors that you've worked with before or crossed paths with. So we'd all be sitting there in our chairs eating our soggy English sandwiches, pumping it up, dressed up like wizards. It was a pleasantly surreal experience.'

The other new face was Bill Nighy as Minister of Magic Rufus Scrimgeour. Nighy seemed almost relieved that he had been cast in *Deathly Hallows*. 'For a while, I thought I would be the only English actor of a certain age who wasn't in a Harry Potter film,' he said.

While the *Deathly Hallows* filming was at its height, an astonishing figure came to light – a figure that would put into sharp relief Emma's place in the entertainment pecking order and her importance in terms of the international film industry. *Vanity Fair* magazine published a list of Hollywood's highest-paid women – the women who earned the most money during the previous year. On the list were the usual suspects: Sandra Bullock – an Emma favourite – earned $20 million; Angelina Jolie made $21 million; Cameron Diaz? Her pay packet was $27 million. But top of the list – Hollywood's highest-paid actress – was Emma Watson. What's more, she came 14th in the overall list of top Hollywood money spinners – the top five were all movie producers with *Transformers* man Michael Bay at number one. She was the youngest person to make that top list. While still in her teens, Emma Watson – cold and wet in a draughty aircraft hangar in Watford – was named the number-one female movie star in the world.

Meanwhile, the second phase of Burberry's new campaign got under way and there were some new faces alongside Emma's in the photoshoot, again done by Mario Testino. One of them was her brother Alex. By this time, the 17-year-old had acquired the tag of 'celebrity sibling'. He'd got a bit part on the Potter film series and now he had a top-line modelling job. 'I never used to care about what I wore, but now Emma will say, "You look scruffy – you're not going to an event in that, are you?" So she will tell me what to wear,' he told the *Daily* Mail. 'We're close, even though she's at uni in the US. She's a positive influence; she's always looking out for my interests.'

Alex had also been signed up by the Storm modelling agency. 'Today is really special for me in a number of different ways,' she said of the shoot. 'It's so nice to see Mario and Christopher again. They also shot my brother in the campaign. He's having such a great time. He's so psyched.'

Emma was pictured sporting a variety of trench coats and clutch bags for the spring/summer campaign and artistic director Christopher Bailey – who'd recently been named British Designer of the Year – was clearly delighted at getting Emma back on board. 'We've worked again with Emma Watson, who has a classic, effortless beauty and is incredibly talented,' he said. 'We wanted this kind of eclectic but very cool crowd of people. We always talk about how much fun we have making these images and I wanted to capture some of the excitement that you feel on set when all these different creative attitudes and personalities come together. Mario has shot these as both stills and video, so we can share some of that energy with a wider audience.'

Thanks to the Emma Effect, Burberry was indeed reaching a wider audience. Since she first became involved the brand had seen profits jump by 23 per cent, in-store sales were up by 16 per cent and the company now had a million followers on Facebook. Financial website This Is Money believed they knew why Burberry was on the up: 'The girl it has to thank, apparently, is the magical Miss Emma Watson,' the site stated. 'Fresh-faced, quietly confident, and world-famous thanks to her role in the Harry Potter films, she has seen the firm's fortunes skyrocket since she starred in its advertising campaigns. That 2008 memory of former soap star and cocaine addict Daniella Westbrook kitted out head-to-toe in Burberry check – a moment which saw demand for the design plummet – can now be filed away under corporate nightmares.'

But some commentators saw a big gap between, on the one hand, Emma and the bright young things pictured in the ads pouting in their ultra-expensive trench coats and, on the other, what regular teenagers would be likely to afford. *Daily Mail* columnist Karen Wheeler clucked her disapproval when the ads appeared: 'Emma is beautiful. She is also clever – she's a student at an Ivy League university in the US – but would she persuade me to buy a Burberry raincoat? The answer is "No". In fact, every time I see the pictures of the actress looking at the camera with a vaguely sullen expression and just a hint of contempt, it makes me not want to buy Burberry. The problem is partly one of credibility. Emma is not long out of her school uniform (albeit a Hogwarts one), while the woman who can afford to spend £800 on a Burberry mac is likely to be in her 40s. Emma looks unconvincing. You just know she'd be much happier dressed in a denim mini, flip-flops and a camisole, like other teens. There has always been a credibility gap in fashion advertising between the women who can afford to wear the clothes and the skinnier, more youthful models who advertise them.'

Emma would soon provide a neat response to detractors who claimed she was out of touch when her 'eco-fashion' range of clothes was unveiled. The 'Love From Emma' collection was created with Fair Trade fashion label People Tree, set up by Safia Minney, who'd recently been awarded an MBE. The clothes were handmade from organic Fair Trade cotton and helped create jobs in India, Bangladesh and Nepal.

Emma was very much the driving force behind the range. She was keen to point out that she hadn't merely allowed People Tree to use her name, though the link up came about by accident. 'It was all because my friend, Alex Nicholls, was wearing this great People Tree T-shirt one day, which I liked. He then told me all about the company – he knows Safia and said that I should meet her. He set up an introduction and Safia and I just clicked. A couple of weeks later, she got in touch with the idea of a teen range – they were doing older ranges and baby clothes but nothing in between – and asked if I'd like to help put it together. I said yes straight away. I wanted to help People Tree produce a younger range because I was excited by the idea of using fashion as a tool to alleviate poverty and knew it was something I could help make a difference with. I think young people like me are becoming increasingly aware of the humanitarian issues surrounding fast fashion and want to make good choices, but there aren't many options out there.'

Emma claimed she essentially designed the kind of clothes she liked to wear. Some of the tops included slogans such as 'Don't Panic, I'm Organic'. 'I have been very heavily involved in the design side, but I don't want to take credit for being a designer as I haven't trained as a designer,' she said. 'I haven't been to art college and I didn't want this collection to be about me, and this is not an Emma Watson clothing line. This is not a celebrity endorsement. This is something I thought was a really great idea and I wanted to help with. I just thought fashion was a great way to help people.'

Photoshoots for the clothes weren't quite on the scale of the Burberry extravaganzas. Young Brit photographer Andrea Carter-Bowman was drafted in to keep things youthful and Emma got friends and family in to do the modelling in Sussex – brother Alex was there along with Emma's old schoolfriend Sophie Sumner. She was a fellow Headingtonian who, like Emma, had been signed up by the Storm modelling agency. She'd even shared Emma's north London flat when she'd moved out of Oxford the previous year. 'It's been really nice to be on the other side of the camera for once,' Emma told *People Tree* magazine. 'I've really enjoyed the styling, planning where we were going to have the shoot, choosing the models, hair and makeup. I chose the location as it had so much within it. There is an orchard, there is a place to have a tea party, there's a swing, beautiful scenery, a lake, plants and flowers. Everything, really, even a vegetable garden. It is the perfect idyllic British summer house, which is what I wanted. The clothes are very British. It's very strawberries and cream and tennis.'

'She worked so, so hard,' Sophie Sumner said. 'After working 13 hours filming, she would get home and sit down and get her designs done.'

The range allowed fashion writers to polish off the usual Potter-related puns. The collection was, according to the *Daily Telegraph*, 'ethical attire that will put a spell on you'. The *Mail on Sunday* was even keener: 'Emma weaves her fashion magic . . . People Tree has some serious fashion cred. Never before has clothing with a conscience felt quite so on trend.' *The Times* took the whole thing a little more seriously: 'What Watson provides is an understanding that a bit of Hollister jersey blended into American Apparel basics, and topped off with humorous slogans, will mean that these clothes can transcend their worthy beginnings – and just become cool.'

The clothes were a hit.

Emma managed to top up her fashion credentials even further that spring with a whistlestop series of events that found her being hailed as Britain's unofficial Ambassador of Fashion. She co-hosted the London Show Rooms initiative event in New York, flying the flag for Brit designers at a party organised by *American Vogue* and the British Fashion Council in an initiative that aimed to increase the profile of British design talent in the US. She wore a Christopher Kane leather-and-lace number that night. 'I hear she gave a little squeak of delight when she tried it on,' Kane told *Vogue*. 'I was really impressed because, let's face it, those dresses are hardcore and not everyone gets the point. Or, more to the point, can pull them off. Emma reminds me of a young Grace Kelly – clean and sophisticated. And, if she's using a stylist, then Emma's the one in control.'

Emma's opinion was now in demand by the America fashionistas as to how she would sum up Britstyle. 'It's so funny because, now that I'm in America, I'm more able to define it,' she told fashion website WWD. 'Before I didn't have an awareness of another style. I think it has to do with the weather. We have terrible weather. It's very grey and drizzly, so we need things to cheer us up. And I think that leads to a lot of creativity and colour, and I think that's why our designers are so innovative. Because at home we're kind of up against the elements in a sense. And we need cheering up. I think we do very well with kind of an eclectic mix. We have great vintage and we love to mix and match: high street and high fashion, vintage . . . and I think that really defines it as well.'

Meanwhile, back at Burberry, there was increasing interest in the models who had taken part in the shoot with Emma . . . and one of them in particular was attracting attention. The so-called 'cool crowd' that Emma was pictured with – as well as brother Alex – comprised model Max Hurd, grandson of former Foreign Secretary Douglas Hurd; Matt Gilmour, son of Pink Floyd guitarist David Gilmour; and 19-year-old Yorkshire musician George Craig. Many of the shots featured Emma up close and personal with Craig. 'I love being part of the family,' Craig said. 'Working with Burberry is obviously an absolute honour.'

'He's an incredibly talented young British musician,' Burberry's Christopher Bailey said. 'I love George's energy and his effortless style. He's also a joy to work with, and it just so happens that he comes from my native Yorkshire in England.'

As lead singer of the band One Night Only, Craig had achieved more attention than success, but his band had generated a buzz, mainly thanks to the support of Radio 1 DJ Jo Wiley, who had taken a shine to the young band's out-of-kilter brand of 80s pop rock. Their single 'Just For Tonight' made the top ten in 2007 and big things were expected of them. A One Night Only track, 'It's Alright', was also used in a video to show off the new Burberry campaign pictures.

Emma would go on to shoot a video for the band's 2010 single 'Say You Don't Want It' in New York. She gets to go on a night on the tiles with George as the band play on a rooftop before the punchline of the story is revealed, just as the singer is leaning in for a kiss. Being an aficionado of classic cartoons, Emma, with George, came up with a storyline, based on the Disney movie *Lady and the Tramp*. 'I play Lady. Lady is a dog from the Upper East Side. She's lost her owner, she's in a dodgy neighbourhood, a bit scared. Then Tramp rocks up and gets her to come along for a ride round New York. Kind of a chance meeting that lasts for a certain period of time, like fleeting and transient, but kind of beautiful and life-changing.'

'It's great to have people like her and people from Burberry and all sorts of really influential people telling people about this really exciting thing we've got going on,' the singer told XFM. 'It's lovely.'

Emma's presence in the video was only enough to push the single to Number 23 in the charts that year, but more people seemed interested in her relationship with George Craig than in the music he and his band were producing. When they were snapped attending a play in June 2010, interest in the pair was increased. Any thought Emma might have had of a low-key visit to see First World War drama *War Horse* were doomed to failure when Craig tweeted, 'Heading to London this afternoon, going to the theatre tonight with a wonderful lady.'

As far as the press were concerned, Emma had dumped

Jay Barrymore to take up with Spanish student Rafael Cebrian. Now she was the 'wonderful lady' on the arm of a young indie-rock singer.

Emma watchers got their confirmation of the couple's relationship when the pair went to the 2010 Glastonbury festival. 'I've just arrived and I'm blown away by the size of the festival,' she told reporters who spotted the pair arriving. 'We only finished filming last week so I'm still trying to get my head round it. I'm here to enjoy myself and plan to see lots of bands.'

George Craig added, 'She wants to be a rock chick after ten years of Harry Potter.'

Craig had played Glastonbury with One Night Only two years earlier. He was keen to see the indie band The Cheek, while Emma had her eye on electro-folkie Imogen Heap – she'd been a longstanding fan.

The pair stood at the side of the stage as American band Vampire Weekend played and created a stir every time they appeared on the festival site. Press photographers roaming the site had a field day that year: Kate Moss and Pixie Geldof were also there.

Emma, wearing shorts and a camouflage corset – Burberry of course – got into the festival spirit by getting a temporary tattoo from the charity WaterAid that featured the words 'Mother Lover'.

Radio 1 DJ Jo Wiley interviewed Emma and George live as part of the station's Glastonbury coverage and cleverly managed to tease a confirmation out of them that they were together, asking them if this was their first date. At first, Emma deferred to George before saying, 'We've been friends since the Burberry shoot. When I was in the States, George was sending me through some of his music as he was recording it. I'm a big fan. I thought everything he did was amazing.'

When the DJ asked them if they had a celebrity couple 'name' yet, along the lines of Brad Pitt and Angelina Jolie (Brangelina) or Tom Cruise and Katie Holmes (TomKat), Emma suggested WatAig.

'You seem very loved up,' Wiley told them. 'It's nice to see you looking so happy together.'

As the end of filming got nearer, there was a chance for Emma to see how Harry Potter would continue after the final films had been and gone. At the end of May, she went to get a sneak preview of the Wizarding World of Harry Potter at Universal Studios in Orlando, Florida. The 20-acre themed area – part of the larger Islands of Adventure park – was due to open the following month and Emma took an early tour of the rides and attractions along with other cast members – including Oliver and James Phelps (the Weasley twins), Matthew Lewis (Neville Longbottom) and, rather incongruously, Robbie Coltrane.

The idea of extending the Potter franchise had entered the story soon after the success of the initial films. The first serious suitors were Disney, who came in with the idea of a standalone theme park totally dedicated to all things Potter. Such a venture would require compromise – but neither Disney nor J. K. Rowling was in the business of compromise and the deal fell through. Universal then stepped in with the idea of giving over a section of their existing park to Harry Potter. Universal were happy to let the author put her stamp on the park – they would re-theme the existing 'Lost Continent' sector of the Islands of Adventure site – and give it the 'Jo Touch'. 'I would have to say a lot of it is going to have the "Jo Touch", because I've been very, very, very involved, which has been amazing,' Rowling told a web chat with fans as the park was being prepared. 'There were a few things that I really wanted to happen if it went ahead. And the key thing for me was if there was to be a theme park that Stuart Craig, who was the production designer on the films, would be involved – more than involved, that he would pretty much design it. Because I love the look of the films, they really mirror what's been in my imagination for all these years. And I just think he's done an incredible job. He's an Oscar-winning, very well-known guy in the industry, so it's not just me who thinks that. And he did consent to get involved, so I truly think that walking into the theme park will be as close as you will ever get to walking on to the film set, or to walking into Hogsmeade. Better, of course, because it's 3D and you can walk around the corner and look at the back. It's going to be quite incredible. I really believe that. Personally, I think it will be the best thing in the world of its type, having seen what I've seen.'

The author got so caught up with the experience when she visited that she bought a huge amount of sweets in the Honeyduke's shop. The shop assistant was unsure whether they should take her money – the author pushed nearly $500 into his hand before walking out with her purchases.

For Emma, the theme park was a surreal notion: it was

one thing to walk into a shop and see yourself as an action figure, quite another to have rides, shops and attractions bearing your face. 'When myself, Daniel and Rupert auditioned,' Emma told *Fault* magazine, 'we had no idea how big it was going to be. We thought we were only making two movies, let alone all the merchandise, fans and now a theme park. It's weird but at the same time cool.'

On her visit, Emma got to see re-creations of key places and themes from the stories, sampling a butterbeer at the Hog's Head pub and some food at the Three Broomsticks. She tried out the Forbidden Journey ride and experienced the sensation of having Moaning Myrtle talk to her as she used the toilet. 'I was not expecting to feel like this. I really wasn't. I was blown away,' Emma said. 'It's really kind of amazing. I've always been a huge fan of the books, aside from the fact that I've been a part of the films, so for me it's just such a pleasure and a delight to see all these things I've read about come to life. A film set has a cut-off point, you know – you're only using a particular section of it – but this is a completely immersive environment. Being here was actually really moving and emotional for me, because I know that the sets are going to come down, but this will be here for ever.'

'Emma and I had a rather emotional moment, actually,' Robbie Coltrane said as he finished the tour, 'because it was kind of like bits of your life suddenly made real.'

The *Sun* newspaper sent travel editor Lisa Minot to take an early look at the attraction. 'After a sneak peek, I can say it is the most faithful re-creation of J. K. Rowling's books and movies ever seen,' she wrote in May 2010. 'From

Moaning Myrtle haunting the toilets to Potter and pals stalking the corridors, fans will be in heaven. The excitement starts the minute you walk through the ornate gates and spy the Hogwarts Express billowing steam at Hogsmeade train station. Snow sparkles on the roofs of village shops, the Three Broomsticks Inn and Hog's Head pub. Hogwarts Castle towers on a grey, rocky crag above a forest of pines. You can pop into Ollivander's Wand Shop or the Owl Post Office and enjoy three great rides. The park features a host of technological firsts and stars of the films are brought to life with state-of-the-art holograms, robotics and live action.'

Back at Leavesden, the final days of Potter filming were approaching. Emma started to wish she'd kept a better record of the last decade. She decided to buy a camera to document the final weeks and days of the extraordinary experience she'd been part of. 'I wandered into a second-hand camera shop, and this very nice gentlemen persuaded me I needed an old black-and-white film camera,' she told *Empire* magazine. 'I realised I hadn't taken any photos for the last ten years, so this time I've been bugging everyone. Takes me about ten minutes to take one because I have to work out the aperture, the shutter speed, the focus and everything. But the girl who was helping me develop the film accidentally turned on the lights in the darkroom and wiped everything. I couldn't talk for about three days. I was devastated. Forget the arty cool effect of using old film cameras. It's absolutely bollocks. Digital cameras and Photoshop is the way to go.'

Saturday, 12 June 2010 would be the last day of filming for the entire Harry Potter series. 'Oh, my goodness! I can't believe this is it,' Emma said, recalling her feelings about that day while talking to the Scholastic website. 'I can't believe this day has finally come. I just thought it would never end, you know? I thought it would never be over. It just felt really strange, so I had to pinch myself. It was pretty weird.'

Producers threw a party and laid on a mariachi band to entertain cast and crew. The young stars reacted in different ways. The terminally easy-going Rupert Grint was by now the proud owner of his very own Mr Whippy ice-cream van. He brought it to the set and served cast and crew with 99s. It served to lighten the mood, but only temporarily. 'The last day, the realisation was overwhelming,' Grint told STV.

Grint spent part of it clearing out his dressing room, where he found toys he used to play with when he started out on the series. The tears were bubbling under. 'It was really emotional. Emma and Dan were the first ones to go, and I just couldn't help it. There was something really empty and final about it – plus the last scene was the most random scene we could have ended on. It was just us jumping through a fireplace, and that was it.'

Emma recalled being slightly disappointed that the whole of the adventure had come to just this, what she described as 'a tiny scene'. 'We were just jumping on to crash mats really, she said. 'It felt very, very strange. Emotional. It felt like a moment in history.'

Filming was finished. Daniel Radcliffe was presented

with his prop glasses from *Deathly Hallows*, as well as the very first pair of glasses he wore as Harry Potter in *Philosopher's Stone*. He marvelled at how tiny they were. 'I would have swiped them if they hadn't given them to me,' he told CNN. 'I absolutely would have stolen them.'

Emma was given a 1957 Rolex watch. Like that presented to any worker retiring from a long-held job, the timepiece had her length of service engraved on the back: 2002–2010. She also approached producers to ask for some mementos of her time in the films – three items in all: 'I asked permission to take Hermione's time turner and her cloak and wand. Those are the three things I took with me.'

David Heyman recalled, 'A few of us gave speeches – Daniel Radcliffe, David Yates and myself.' Heyman's speech nearly ground to a halt as emotion got the better of him. 'It was very moving. We all talked about how it's like being part of the family. It was very intimate and lovely.'

Director David Yates told *USA Today* how the enormity of what was about to happen kicked in as the final moments came closer. 'I don't think we ever took it for granted. We'd sometimes joke about what we're going to do when it's all over. We'll never have this amount of resources again. We're going to have to go back into the real world, after living in this bubble.'

Then a film was shown to the cast and crew. Put together by an assistant director, it was a behind-the-scenes compilation of scenes and moments from the series along with messages and goodbyes from people who couldn't be there. The film ended with an as-yet-unseen trailer for the new film, but by that stage the damage was done. Emma began to weep. 'I'm the girl, it was obviously me – I was the first to crack,' she told Radio 1. 'Then Dan, then Rupert went, then we were all just a mess.'

The three young actors put their arms around each other as they wept. 'I think the fact that there's two other people in the world who've shared this unique experience makes you feel less alone,' Emma said.

Daniel Radcliffe remembered, 'I've never seen Rupert Grint cry before; it was weird. It was like seeing your dad cry.'

Then it was gone. The filming world that had provided Emma with wealth, fame and a consistency that she lacked in her own life was over. The Watford World of Harry Potter was no more, gone, apart from one gesture of nostalgia and friendship organised by Emma by way of a thank-you and a goodbye. Emma invited the key young cast members to her home in north London. 'I threw a dinner,' she told the Scholastic website. 'I just bought a new apartment in London. I tried to make it look really nice. I bought tons of flowers. I lit candles everywhere and everyone had place settings and I made food for everyone to come and eat. I made a book for everyone and I had silly questions like: Who was your first crush on the set? What was your best memory? What was your worst memory? Who was your favourite director? Stuff like that, that's just really fun. And everyone had a piece of paper to write it all down, but we all discussed our answers and went around and listened to people's stories and what they remembered. It was just a really nostalgic evening, basically, just all of us sharing stories. It was a really nice evening and it was warm weather, so we sat outside as well, and I bought disposable cameras for the tables, so everyone could use those, and it was just fun. It was just . . . chill.'

ELEVEN

HONESTLY! I JUST HAD A HAIRCUT

The Harry Potter filming saga was finally over with – at least that was what Emma thought. Other than her university commitments, she had an unusually large chunk of free time ahead of her. 'I'm not planning to do an awful lot this summer,' Emma said in mid-2010. 'I'll take a bit of a break and enjoy that, really.'

Of course, she did no such thing. She went to Dhaka, the capital of Bangladesh, with People Tree founder Safia Minney to see for herself if the Fair Trade approach to fashion and manufacture could really make a difference. The trip was the logical flowering of the seeds of social consciousness sown by her Headington geography teacher during her A levels – to see if the Fair Trade concept really worked.

After a hair-raising car journey through the streets of Dhaka – all heat, noise and driving unrestrained by the niceties of the Highway Code – Emma and Safia went to a clothes factory in the city's slum district. Looking pale and shocked, Emma was given a tour of the area as scores of children looked on at the strange visitor wearing a light red, sari-style dress. Workers there were being paid the equivalent of £6 per week and were campaigning to get wages brought up to around £18.

'We visited the slums in Dhaka,' Emma said, 'where the garment-factory workers live. I had some preconceived ideas but nothing prepared me for the reality. It was upsetting to see the conditions in which these people live, but I was incredibly moved by their spirit and friendliness in spite of such apparent adversity. Facilities? There are no facilities there to speak of. In the building we visited, I saw one shower, one cleaning place and one hole in the floor, which was the toilet. This was for the whole floor. That floor had maybe eight or nine rooms coming off it, and each room housed a whole family, that is 32 people to one toilet.'

People Tree filmed Emma in the slums and the crew interviewed one female worker who made the reality of her situation clear to the young actress. 'She was very candid about the fact that there just wasn't any hope for her,' Emma said. 'There is no hope for anyone living in those conditions and being paid that kind of wage.'

She also met with the head of the national Garment Workers Federation before moving on to a Fair Trade centre called Swallows in the Thanapara region, which had created jobs for 200 women. As well as clothes manufacture at Swallows, there was a day-care centre and a school for 300 children. The school was open to workers and to people from the wider area, an illustration of the trickle-down effect of Fair Trade policies.

Emma helped the children with their maths and acted as a teacher's assistant, gathering in their work. She even took a turn on a foot-driven sewing machine and watched as workers dyed and wove yarn, cut it into patterns, sewed it and embroidered it. 'It is so hard for people to imagine what it takes to create something and how special that item of clothing is,' she said. 'Coming to Swallows I see that there is an alternative. The living conditions are modest but it's clean and there is a real sense of community, their families are together and they seem to love and be proud of what they're doing – many things that we in the West take for granted. Swallows is special and I need to believe for my own peace of mind that there will be more places like this in the developing countries in the world.'

The Bangladesh video would be among the last images that people would see of the 'old' Emma. 'New' Emma was about to appear. On 5 August at 4.57pm, Emma posted a picture of herself on Facebook. It caused a sensation. It also neatly sidestepped the chance of any paparazzi snatching pictures of her and making money from them – she was clearly in control of the situation. The picture of an elfin-looking, very short-haired Emma – *very* short-haired – was followed by a brief status update: 'Dear all. Cut my hair off a few days ago . . . Feels incredible. I love it. I've wanted to do this for years and years; it's the most liberating thing ever. Hope you like. Big love from Emma x.'

Not since Britney Spears went to work with a pair of electric clippers in 2007 would one haircut spark off so much interest and debate. 'At that moment I felt I became a woman,' she told the *Sun*. 'I'm ready to start taking risks.'

Ever since she was young, Emma's appearance had been largely dictated by her filming commitments. At a time when most young girls were trying out different styles and looks, Emma was not allowed to. 'For the nine years I was on Harry Potter, I was contractually obliged not to cut my hair, not to tan – all the normal things girls do, I couldn't,' she told *Vogue*. 'So, when I got the chance to change my appearance – this is what I did. I didn't realise until afterwards how significant it was because of course the hair was Hermione's defining feature. It's my way of being myself.'

She had spoken many times – especially to her dad, Chris – about wanting to change her appearance, and particularly her hair, saying she wanted to do something different, and cut it all off. While carrying out press duties in New York, she walked into the Cutler Salon. She hadn't told anyone where she was going and went in alone. In her hand was a picture of actress Mia Farrow, with the boyishly short haircut she had sported in the 1960s. She showed it to hairdresser Rodney Cutler and said, 'I want to look like this. Make it happen.'

Cutler was clearly in his element – the Australian-born crimper was keen on shorter cuts. 'Some of my favourite hairstyles are the graduated bob, as seen on Louise Brooks in the twenties, which is timeless,' he told the *Beauty Interviews* website. 'Linda Evangelista's short haircut at the height of her career – that set the tone for what was hot in hair fashion.'

Grabbing a ponytail full of her hair, he set to work. 'It was weird,' Emma recalled. 'My hairdresser was like, "When are you going to freak out? Most people cry or go into shock,"' she told *Entertainment Weekly*. 'But I was very calm. I knew it was the right thing.'

She left the salon alone – and prepared herself for the comments and criticisms that would inevitably follow. 'I knew everyone was going to have an opinion and I couldn't deal with it. I have to get myself into a good place to deal with people saying things like, "It's terrible! She looks like a boy!"

'I'm 20 now, so I'm not a child any more,' she told the *Daily Mail*. 'I've been on Harry Potter for ten years now, so I felt the need to mark the end of it in some way – I needed some way to say to myself, "Right, you're entering a new phase of your life now. I needed a change." And that's what the haircut is about.'

Dad Chris soon heard about the haircut. 'He was away when I had it done and I got this phone call . . . Emma, what have you done? He said don't get carried away – you're not Audrey Hepburn yet. He loves it now. He's eating his words.'

Column inches across the world were filled with opinion about Emma's new look – there were 16,000 comments and 'likes' on her Facebook page and she would be near the top of most fashion writers' most-stylish list by the end of the year. Hair experts were drafted in to the debate to give their opinions on her makeover and whether anyone could get away with the 'Emma Pixie Cut'. 'She is clearly making a big style statement and experimenting with her hair and look,' said Toni & Guy international artistic director Cos Sakkas. 'It strikes me as a coming of age and mature step away from her long pretty look and embraces something far edgier that opens her up to new acting roles. Of course, with an extreme short cut like this you need the facial features to pull it off – which Emma clearly has,' he added.

'Emma Watson's new super-short pixie crop is perfection,' said British Hairdresser of the Year Mark Woolley. 'It's cute, playful and a touch rebellious, and has totally updated her style. The soft layers in Emma's hair emphasise her pretty, delicate features beautifully. Channelling the look of the sixties, she's clearly leading the way with a style which will be one of the biggest hair trends this autumn.'

Despite taking the initiative with her online postings, Emma was indeed snapped by the paparazzi, crossing a New York street, but she'd taken the sting out of their value by jumping the gun on the press. Emma's Potter co-stars were also dragged into the debate. 'Emma had sort of hinted that she was going to do that,' Daniel Radcliffe told the Scholastic website. 'So I wasn't as surprised as perhaps the rest of the world was, but I think she looks fantastic. It's a very, very cool haircut. But, to be honest, the girl could look pretty with a plastic bag over her head, you know. I mean, she's a beautiful girl, so any haircut I'm sure would look wonderful.'

Many commentators were looking for deep psychological

reasons why she would do something so drastic. They even claimed she'd done it to win the part of Lisbeth Salander in a forthcoming remake of the Swedish film *The Girl with the Dragon Tattoo*. To Emma, though, the reason was a simple one: 'I haven't been able to change my hair for ten years. Some people don't like it, they think it's an outward expression of my inner torment, my Britney Spears moment. Honestly! I just had a haircut.'

But some commentators thought that the timing of the 'The Haircut' was about something else. At the very time she grabbed the headlines with the pixie cut, it was claimed another chop was taking place. EMMA WATSON AXED BY BURBERRY, said the headlines – on the very day that Emma's cropped picture was released on Facebook.

Despite a 23 per cent jump in Burberry profits after she started working with the brand, it was claimed that she was being replaced by model and face about town Rosie Huntington-Whiteley. The 20-year-old had been voted *Elle*'s Model of the Year in 2009 and had already worked for Ralph Lauren, DKNY and lingerie firm Victoria's Secret. She'd also established herself as a tabloid favourite as the girlfriend of action-movie star Jason Statham. Just to add more showbiz spice, Huntington-Whiteley had just been cast as Megan Fox's replacement in the new *Transformers* movie. The company's creative director Christopher Bailey was diplomatic: 'Emma is a big part of the Burberry family and is also a wonderful friend . . . I have huge admiration for her both personally and professionally and everything she's achieved.'

But 'The Haircut' and her changing relationship with

Burberry did little to dent Emma's popularity. Shortly afterwards, she was voted the sexiest British actress under the age of 30, beating the likes of Sienna Miller, Keira Knightley and Emily Blunt. She was clearly doing something right.

But the darker side of fame reared its head again for Emma in 2010 when a court in Manchester banned a 38-year-old man from contacting her for five years after he superimposed pictures of the actress's face on to indecent images of children. John Cavanagh was found to have 2,000 images of Emma on his computer when police called at his flat in Didsbury, south Manchester. He also had 1,300 indecent images on his laptop and in some pictures Emma's face had been spliced together with those pictures. He'd also doctored pictures from Harry Potter films, replacing Daniel Radcliffe's face with his own to make it look like he was sharing the scene with Emma.

Police – who came to the flat to talk about non-payment of rent – also found an indecent picture of a young girl lying on top of a pile of soft toys in a wardrobe. They also found games wrapped as presents and a 'dossier' of women he knew with young children. Judge Anthony Hammond gave Cavanagh a three-year community order with three years' supervision and an order to attend a sex-offender programme. He was also told to have no contact with Emma or use the Internet for anything other than applying for a job.

In court, the judge said, '[Of] the images I have seen ... The few that purport to show the actress Emma Watson are crude images and not the sort of thing that would have, in my view, any commercial value. There is no evidence that you have been spreading these around. These are pathetic images kept for your own purposes. You are not allowed to have them because quite simply children are harmed in the making of these photographs.'

It was another example of the kind of unwanted, disturbing attention someone as high profile as Emma could attract. There would be more. Fake pictures of her started being passed around from computer to computer at Brown. It's believed they 'showed' Emma topless with a towel round her waist. A spokesperson for Emma told the *Daily Mail*, 'There have been a number of nude fakes over the past two months. Emma has seen them and finds them tiresome. People should know better.'

While this was going on, the film industry was caught by surprise by a change of heart on *Deathly Hallows*. It had been announced that the first part would be released in 3D, despite the fact that it hadn't been shot in that format. It was then announced that the producers had changed their minds. The film industry had experienced a shot in the arm thanks to 3D. The Film Distributors' Association believed that cinemagoers donning their glasses had increased overall box-office takings by 8 per cent so far in 2010, with the top three films all appearing in the 3D format. But there had been criticism of studios 'converting' 2D into three dimensions to cash in on the trend – reviewers were particularly scathing about sword-and-sorcery film *Clash of the Titans*, which had been released in April after undergoing conversion.

By sticking to 2D, the studio behind the Potter films

were potentially losing out on a bumper payday – tickets for 3D films are more expensive – but saving some credibility among film fans. 'Despite everyone's best efforts, we were unable to convert the film in its entirety and meet the highest standards of quality,' a statement from Warner Brothers said. 'We do not want to disappoint fans who have long anticipated the conclusion of this extraordinary journey. We, in alignment with our filmmakers, believe this is the best course to take in order to ensure that our audiences enjoy the consummate Harry Potter experience.'

As the final touches were being made to the very two-dimensional version of *Deathly Hallows*, Emma returned to America and to Brown. But she still had work to do: there was a new film to promote as well as voice recording for the second *Deathly Hallows* to be done. The end of Potter was proving to be a slower one than Emma was expecting. It was, in her words, a 'gradual goodbye' and her feelings about her 'release' were mixed to say the least. 'I go through periods where it feels fine, easy, and I'm busy at school,' she said. 'Then there are days when I feel really lost, because it was just so structured and I had people telling me where I needed to be, what they wanted me to do. My whole life was on a schedule, on a call sheet, every day, and, being at university, you decide when you eat, where you go, if you work, if you don't. No one cares and it's all down to you.

'So, yeah, I had days where I feel "Oof", but it was always going to be an adjustment, and I feel lucky that I kept going with school and that I have that kind of infrastructure to fall back on. It feels nice to be able to take a bit of a break. Making these two films back to back was exhausting, I mean really exhausting. I was hanging in rags when we finished shooting.'

The British press got their first up-close glance at the new-look Emma Watson on 10 November 2010 – not at a Potter premiere but at a film-industry event in central London. The party at Claridge's was to celebrate ambitious plans to rejuvenate Leavesden Studios, the spiritual home of the Harry Potter franchise. Warner Brothers had announced their decision to buy the site earlier in the year. Despite the billions generated by the Potter films and the fact that new films had been attracted to the studios thanks to their success, the former aircraft factory had seen better days. As part of the £100 million renovations, two new soundstages would be built to preserve the sets – so lovingly made by designer Stuart Craig – that had been used in the Potter saga. Tantalisingly for Potter fans, it was also announced that behind-the-scenes tours of the soundstages were planned to start in 2012. That news went down very well with the huge online community of fans worldwide.

Barry Meyer, chairman of Warner Brothers, told the *Watford Observer* – the studios' local paper – that the revamp would create hundreds of jobs. 'We are going to have one of the largest, most technologically advanced film production studios in all of Europe. We've been around for 85 years so we are not in this for the short term. Any ideas of that should be dispelled by the fact that we've just invested a substantial amount of money in buying the studio.'

The Claridge's event was attended by all the young Potter stars, but all eyes – and cameras – were on Emma. This may have been because of the striking black dress she wore. It may have been because of the fact that, despite the swanky surroundings, Daniel Radcliffe and Rupert Grant decided to turn up in T-shirts and jeans. But it was mainly to do with the fact that she looked like a movie star and they didn't – and she had 'The Haircut' and was giving it its first red-carpet outing. She wore a striking, one-sleeved black cocktail dress from the new Vionnet collection with a pearl-encrusted necklace and a red poppy pin at the waist to mark Remembrance Day.

'The three of us have spent the last ten years of our lives at Leavesden Studios,' Daniel told reporters. 'To suddenly see it as the centre of all this attention is amazing. It's an amazing resource in this country for tens of thousands of incredibly talented writers and producers, filmmakers and actors. Warner Brothers has done a huge amount to release that talent into the world.'

Emma added that she'd had 'the time of my life making films at Leavesden Studios'.

As the Claridge's party continued, fans began to camp out – literally erect tents in Leicester Square – in preparation for the premiere of *Harry Potter and the Deathly Hallows Part 1*. Good thing they had come prepared, as, once again, the British weather unleashed its worst on a Potter premiere.

Emma didn't disappoint the waiting photographers,

wearing a black-lace minidress designed by Rafael Lopez. The ultra-short, see-though, feathered outfit – costing around £4,000 – was topped off with earrings by Solange Azagury-Partridge and black heels by Charlotte Olympia. There was one other fashion item that Emma brought into play: sticky tape to stop the tiny dress falling open at the back. There would be no wardrobe malfunctions this time around. There were other stars there that night, but only one person grabbed the headlines the following day: EMMA WATSON STUNS IN BLACK LACE DRESS AT HARRY POTTER PREMIERE, said the *Daily Mail*.

The *Daily Telegraph*'s fashion pages agreed: 'A stunning Emma Watson bewitched fans at the premiere of the penultimate Harry Potter film, *Harry Potter and the Deathly Hallows Part 1*, in London last night. Arriving at Leicester Square to greet an army of fans, the 20-year-old actress left little to the imagination in a revealing minidress by Spanish-born designer Rafael Lopez. If there was only one message intended by "that dress", it's that Emma Watson, in all her grown-up, drop-dead-gorgeous fashionista glory, has arrived.'

The fashion blitz was intensified for the New York premiere. Emma wore a floor-length black dress especially designed for her. 'I asked Calvin Klein Collection if they would make a dress for me because I love their stuff, and they did,' she told reporters outside the Alice Tully Hall in Manhattan. Emma's fashion sense even seemed to rub off a little on her co-stars; Daniel Radcliffe and Rupert Grint – not normally known for grabbing the headlines with what they wore – were kitted out in Dolce and Gabbana suits.

Emma's 'date' for the premiere was her brother Alex. Musician George Craig was nowhere to be seen. 'I hate to disappoint everyone,' she told *Vogue*, 'but we're not dating. He's in England, I'm in America . . . There is no one at the moment.'

Questions for Emma also centred on 'The Haircut' – journalists wanted to know if even more dramatic transformations were to follow. 'The hair is as dramatic as it goes,' she said. 'I think I'd have to shave it to get any more dramatic. I'm loving it, I don't really miss it [her old hairstyle]. I'm not going to lie. I can wash my head, in a basin, in a sink. Takes me, like, five minutes to get ready. It's great.'

Sex and the City star Sarah Jessica Parker attended the event with husband Matthew Broderick – Emma's co-star in *The Tale of Despereaux* – and son James, and Emma spent time chatting to the youngster. 'Her son is a big Harry Potter fan,' Emma said. 'We've spoken on a number of occasions. She's a big fashion icon of mine.'

Things had definitely changed since her first Potter premiere nine years earlier. Emma gave fashion writers a lot to fill their columns with while promoting the film in New York. As she dashed from one TV show to another, she donned a dazzling array of outfits: a Burberry trench coat with studded sleeves one minute, then a grey Carven outfit, next an ink-blot Dion Lee minidress. Her fashion sense was news on both sides of the Atlantic: EMMA WATSON'S NEW YORK FASHION SHOW: HARRY POTTER STAR BRINGS HER SWEET STYLE TO THE BIG APPLE, said the *Daily Mail*.

The fashion journalists were happy – but what about the

film reviewers? The first part of the *Deathly Hallows* saga has something for everyone: chases, wand shoot-outs, young men in lacy bras, house-elf murder and topless snogging. 'This is the last Harry Potter story and I really wanted to do it justice and go out with a bang,' Emma said. 'And I was blown away – it was above and beyond all of my expectations.'

Ron and Hermione have to make huge sacrifices to be with Harry and help him fulfil his destiny and continue the work of Dumbledore. Emma explained the thrust of the plot to ITV1's Ben Shephard: 'Voldemort has split his soul into seven different pieces and he's hidden these pieces in seven different objects, which have personal meaning to him. So the only way to defeat Voldemort is to destroy each and every one of these "Horcruxes".'

The three must go on the road as outlaws, but not without leaving behind the worlds they are used to – that includes Hogwarts and, in Hermione's case, her family. This key early scene clearly resonated with Emma: 'The film opens with Hermione wiping her parents' memories [of her] and leaving their house,' she told *Empire*. 'You don't read that in the book – you just know she does it. That's a scene that Steve [Kloves, scriptwriter] and Dave [Yates, director] wrote for the film, which I was happy about because you see the sacrifice that Hermione and Ron make to be Harry's friend. You see Ron's home and Harry's. But you never really get a sense of Hermione's life outside Hogwarts, outside that friendship, and it's important.

'She's not just going off to school for another year. You're choosing between family and friends; it's pretty brutal. They offer her a cup of tea, completely unaware that anything's about to happen, and then I cast a spell that wipes their memories of me. There're photos all around the room, actual childhood pictures of me, and they just dissolve. It's horrible. And then I have to shut the door and walk out alone.'

Unfortunately, the other key non-Rowling scene – the sequence between Harry and Hermione as they dance to the Nick Cave song 'O Children' – just doesn't work. Well intentioned though it is at reinforcing the friendship between the two, it's an awkward and unhelpful watch. It generated a few stifled giggles at some showings.

But there is one sequence in *Deathly Hallows* that definitely does work – and that stands alone among the entire Potter series: *The Tale of the Three Brothers*. This striking shadow-puppet-style animation was directed by Swiss-born Ben Hibon and in this 'film within a film' is narrated by Emma.

The story is of three brothers who think they've cheated death after using magic to cross a river, and the sequence explains the existence of three magical objects – a wand, a stone and a cloak – that make up the Deathly Hallows. It acts as a self-contained morality play and the three-minute sequence can be happily watched on its own – it's also beautifully told by Emma. Director David Yates explained, 'It started with Stuart Craig [production designer on the Potter films] who came up with these wonderful puppet images – shadow puppets. And then we found this wonderful chap called Ben Hibon. He's a really gifted animator whose work we loved and we wanted to develop that shadow-puppet idea with him and he went away and supervised that whole thing for us and did an absolutely beautiful job. He's a very clever man.'

The sequence not only leaves you wanting more, it also solidifies *Deathly Hallows* as the film that asks the most of Emma – she runs, she jumps, she's tortured and she leads the puzzle-solving from the front. It certainly seemed to be a view shared by the man who had put Emma through so much during filming – director David Yates: 'I think she's *ignited*. I think something happened during the filming of *Part 1*. She's always been quite clever and she's always been very thoughtful about how she approaches the acting that she does and she was like that on Five and on Six. She's actually really an intensely bright person. But what I think happened on this one is she started to appreciate how she could tap into an emotional level and tune into things, which most great actors do. They just tap into the stuff inside and she started to do that and it was really exciting when she did.'

Emma agreed: 'Parts of my personality have slipped into Hermione, and lots of her personality I'm sure unconsciously have affected me. I think this Hermione is the closest to my personality. David [Yates] wanted a really honest performance. Earlier on I think I played, like, a parody of myself. She was just this big personality – she's developed into something much more human.'

By this stage in the series, film reviewers were in an unusual position: no matter how damning the critical reaction to the film was, it was unlikely to affect its commercial performance. Even the most hard-hearted critic seemed largely to hold up their hands and surrender. '*Harry Potter and the Deathly Hallows Part 1* is easily the best movie in the series, if only because it's the one movie with the most narrative thrust,' said *Premiere*. 'The entire movie is one long chase sequence, as Harry and his friends slowly become adults under the grimmest of circumstances. The movie is grittier and darker than past episodes, which is a welcome tonal shift. Along the way, the movie provides a number of superb set pieces including Harry's adopted family of friends serving themselves up as bait during a thrilling escape scene. There is an equally thrilling break-in of the Ministry of Magic where our heroes magically make themselves look like middle-aged slobs. A hallucinatory sequence where Harry and Hermione embrace sans clothes will probably be remembered as a moment of sexual awakening for millions. There's also a lovely animated scene that tells a folk tale essential to the story.'

The *Daily Telegraph* observed, 'J. K. Rowling's plot hands the film a gift: it transfers the trio from the stifling environment of Hogwarts to a bigger, broader world. Watching Harry, Hermione and Ron on Shaftesbury Avenue, in the Dartford Tunnel, on cliff tops and deserted beaches makes them more insecure and vulnerable, recalling the children they were in the first films. They buttress a likeable trio of actors now on the cusp of adulthood. Watson and Grint especially are extended as never before: Hermione, once a faintly unappealing little swot, emerges as a bright, brave, resourceful young woman.'

This being a Potter film, though, the praise could never be universal: 'The lead actors do things they've never done before – Radcliffe and Watson share a topless clinch (no wand-flashing, thankfully), while Grint has to play jealousy and paranoia,' said *Empire*. 'But there's no real sense of weight to the breaking of this fellowship. And an invented-for-the-movie scene in which Harry and Hermione enjoy a dance inside their tent is both baffling and cringey. What should feel fresh and urgent, a cross-country chase flick, is bogged down for long stretches by a curse of *Excrucius Overplottio*. J. K. Rowling had the luxury of hundreds of pages to explain it all; delivered as movie exposition, it makes you yearn for the chuck-a-ring-in-a-volcano simplicity of *The Lord of the Rings*.'

By this stage in the game, Emma was an old hand at dealing with the critics. 'I will look back on this part of my life and I know it will be special, but it used to be that, if I ever had a bad review or someone said, "Oh, she is too this," or "She's too that," I got upset about it,' Emma told *The Times*. 'Now what I have worked out is that it would actually be physically impossible to be perfect for everyone. Everyone has a distinct idea in their head of what each character is like. So I've kind of had to lower my standards. I can't be perfect for everyone. J. K. thinks I'm perfect, and that's good enough for me.'

With public interest satisfied as to how the story would be split into two parts, attention now turned to the upcoming conclusion: 15 July 2011 was the date set for the final film's release. 'The very last one's a big old epic, with lots of battles and dragons and goblins,' director David

Yates told *USA Today*. It's going to be operatic. And then it's over.'

The opening weekend for *Deathly Hallows Part 1* proved that, despite any critical misgivings, the public's appetite for all things Potter was undiminished. The film took more than £6 million on the first day of release in Britain; it then took $61 million on its opening day in America, breaking records on both sides of the Atlantic. *Deathly Hallows Part 1* was set to be the most successful Potter yet.

The juggernaut just seemed to get bigger – indeed, *Guinness World Records* confirmed that the Harry Potter series would be named as the highest-grossing film series of all time in its 2011 edition, beating the James Bond franchise, which had been running for more than 40 years longer than the Potter movies. The first six of the Potter films had earned £3.38 billion; all 22 James Bond movies had made a mere £2.29 billion.

Meanwhile, Emma's long goodbye to the series was just about to get a little longer. It was revealed that a key sequence at London's Kings Cross station would have to be reshot. Filmmakers had done the initial shoot in a rush. The sequence included the makeup shots required to make the young stars look older. 'We had two days at Kings Cross . . . and we needed so much more time than that,' she told journalists at a *Hallows* press junket when the news was announced. 'So we have to reshoot at Christmas. It's not over yet.'

The scene called for Emma and the other young stars – including Bonnie Wright as Ron's sister Ginny – to return to Kings Cross for the film's epilogue. This time, filming was shifted to Leavesden to avoid the time pressure of filming on location. For Emma, this meant one thing: another trip to the Leavesden wig department to cover up her chic cropped hairstyle. 'Currently at Leavesden filming reshoots with Dan and Rupert,' she posted on her Facebook page. 'Feels strange to be back!'

Despite the anti-climax of having to return to the studios after the high emotion of the 'final' day of shooting in the summer, it was perhaps fitting that the epilogue sequence eventually became the true finale to the Potter saga, instead of Emma and her co-stars jumping out of a fireplace, as had previously been the case.

Hermione and Ron are now husband and wife; so are Harry and Ginny. They return to Platform Nine and Three-Quarters to see their children off as they journey to Hogwarts. The story – and the filming – had come full circle. 'For me, it almost felt like a real cycle, because I started on that same platform, at the same age that Lily Potter, the youngest daughter of Ginny and Harry, was, so it's almost literally like looking back at myself,' Bonnie Wright told *Total Film*. 'The three kids who played the children were just . . . they just epitomised all of us, when we were that age, so it was lovely to look back. They were so excited on the day – it was a massive dream come true and they'd been through such a massive process of auditioning. I think it was probably the most auditions any person has been through to get a part in a film.'

Emma helped choose the three children used in the film along with the other young stars, so they could act like real families. 'That was definitely a challenge,' Emma said. 'There's so many challenges in these last two. Pretending that I had kids and acting as if they were my children was the weirdest thing . . . that I had *children*. So weird. That was a struggle. I was like, "Am I doing this right? How do I . . .?" It was hard to know how to approach it, so I hope it looks good in the end.'

Bonnie Wright explained, 'The dynamic is incredibly important to try to portray the idea that they are this family unit, that they've spent every living moment together, since they were babies in their hands, to how they are now. It was challenging to get that warmth with someone you've barely met and some children don't want to get close to someone they don't know. But they understood it was incredibly important to make the scene work, so they were very giving to the situation.'

With the epilogue scenes shot, it really was the end. Immediately, people wanted to know what was next for Emma Watson. 'I really want to write a novel,' she told the *Sun*, ideas tumbling out of her. 'I also want to learn to play the mandolin. I have acting projects coming up and I'm in a fantastic position right now. I realise I'm a pretty lucky person and I'm determined to make the most of life – but also to take a few chances if I can.'

The wish she'd made over Sunday lunch all those years earlier had given her everything and more than she could ever have hoped for. The school-hall audition that Emma had wanted so badly had taken her around the world. And the little girl with the big teeth, big, brown, bushy hair and a very bossy voice – created on a train by J. K.

Rowling – was finally left behind at Leavesden Studios. 'I love Hermione with all my heart – I don't think I will ever play a character I identify with so much,' Emma said. 'She's wonderful – smart, brave, determined and loyal. She's just *it*.'

TWELVE

I WISH I'D DONE MORE NAUGHTY THINGS

Harry Potter filming may well have finished, but Emma's acting career definitely hadn't. Despite the hints she'd dropped in previous years – and despite the knowledge that she need never work again – Emma threw herself into a fresh film project.

Speculation had been buzzing about the first post-Potter film choice Emma would make. As a result, she'd already been linked to several upcoming films. One story had her agreeing to appear in the coming-of-age drama *The Perks of Being a Wallflower*. Then she was being linked to sci-fi franchise-in-the-making *Incarceron* alongside *Twilight* star Taylor Lautner. There was even talk of Emma's reuniting with that other *Twilight* star Robert Pattinson – who had played Cedric Diggory in Potter – in a remake of the 2005 art-house comedy *Dark Arc*.

In the end, a very different project caught her eye. She'd

been given a script to read while on a trip to France. 'I was coming back from a photoshoot in Paris on the train,' she explained during press interviews for *Deathly Hallows*. 'I was exhausted and the last thing I wanted to do was read a script. My agent called me up and said, "*Please* just read the script, you won't regret it." I *so* didn't want to, but the minute I opened it up I couldn't put it down. The part was small but really interesting and had a really good character arc; and it was well formed, even though the character only had a few scenes. I called back and said, "You're right . . . I love it."'

The script was for a film called *My Week with Marilyn*. It was based on a book and a published diary recalling the late Colin Clark's memories of acting as a 'gofer' on the 1957 film *The Prince and the Showgirl*, starring Laurence Olivier and Marilyn Monroe. The first book was *The Prince, the Showgirl and Me*; it was followed by *My Week with Marilyn*, which purported to fill in what happened to Clark during nine days unaccounted for in the original publication. Clark's brother – the famed politician and diarist Lord (Alan) Clark – had suggested that the diaries had been fabricated, something Colin Clark denied before his death in 2002.

The project had several connections to Emma's previous projects – unsurprising, as she'd already worked with the cream of film and television talent. *My Week with Marilyn*'s director, Simon Curtis, had made the BBC's 1999 adaptation of *David Copperfield*, which had featured a very young Daniel Radcliffe. Curtis had also worked on the BBC's *Cranford*, written by *Ballet Shoes* scriptwriter Heidi Thomas. Kenneth Branagh – Gilderoy Lockhart himself – had been cast as Laurence Olivier. 'I don't play Marilyn: Michelle Williams plays Marilyn,' Emma said. 'That woman's got serious guts to do that. The film is about Colin Clark, who was a runner on one of her movies, and they had this kind of . . . thing. But at the beginning of the movie he falls for the wardrobe assistant – *moi* – then he runs off with Marilyn and dumps me for a while. He gets older and wiser, comes back and begs for forgiveness.'

Emma's character – the wardrobe assistant Lucy – is described by Clark as 'one of the prettiest little girls I have ever seen in my life . . . slim as a wand, curly brown hair, huge brown eyes and a wide cheeky grin.'

The curly brown hair was clearly an issue for the post-haircut Emma. 'I had to wear a wig,' she sighed. 'I tried up until the last minute to convince Simon Curtis that she had short hair – but he said it was too sophisticated. So I had to wear a wig.'

Emma clearly created a strong impression on Curtis as he made his feature-film debut. 'It's great to have given Emma her first job after Harry Potter,' he told the *Daily Mail*. 'She's a proper actress.'

The real-life Colin and Lucy had carried out their romance on the set of *The Prince and the Showgirl* at Pinewood Studios – the very place where *My Week with Marilyn* was being made. The film was being produced by the Weinstein Company, and studio boss Harvey Weinstein was clearly an Emma fan too. 'For ten years, she has been this schoolgirl in the Harry Potter films and now you see her as a woman for the first time,' he told show-business journalist Baz Bamigboye. 'She has an elegance about her – she looks like [1960s model] Jean Shrimpton. Plus, she has a gift for comedy and drama, and we're just starting to see her range. I feel we're going to work together a lot in the future.'

Emma's post-Potter life was clearly proving to be a busy one: as well as finishing her studies at Brown, there would be the international round of promotional activities for *Deathly Hallows Part 2*. She was also drafted in to promote the DVD and Blu-Ray releases of *Part 1* by making a video asking fans to vote for what artwork they thought should grace the covers. Meanwhile, *The Perks of Being a Wallflower* began to move slowly from the backburner to the front as Emma's connection with the project pushed it closer to actually being made. The film was based on the book of the same name written by Stephen Chbosky. The story is told through a series of letters written by a shy but intelligent teenager called Charlie, observing but not truly participating in life at his high school. The book's tales of teen sex, teen drugs and teen suicide struck a chord with – unsurprisingly – a young audience when it was published in 1999. Just to shore up the book's teen-cool credentials, it was published by MTV Books.

Charlie has only two real friends at school, Patrick and Sam (Samantha). Emma was being lined up to play the part of Sam. Chbosky was going to direct too and he was all too aware of how important casting was. 'Everyone has their own version of what the book is,' he told Shooting Stars website. 'Their own version of what Charlie looks like, and Sam looks like, and Patrick, what he looks and sounds like. That's what I love about books so much. It involves the reader so deeply. So all the movie can ultimately be is my version of it, you know, and I hope that people who love the book can get a little bit more insight. Because it is the book, but there are certain little differences that I hope they find interesting.'

Summit Entertainment – the company behind the *Twilight* series – came on board to produce the film and Emma's co-star was named as Logan Lerman, best known for the fantasy movie *Percy Jackson and the Lightning Thief*. As ever, there was a connection with Emma's previous life: *Percy Jackson* had been directed by Chris Columbus. On 10 February 2011, Emma ended the speculation by confirming on Facebook and Twitter that she was committed to appearing in the film. 'Hi everyone, I just wanted to let you know that the rumours are true – I'm going to be playing Sam in *The Perks of Being a Wallflower* opposite Logan Lerman.'

Emma's commitment to the project was likely to have been a major factor in its coming to fruition. What's more, the drugs, sex and suicide to be found in the source material were the key indicator to how her career was going to be heading: after the period-piece glam of *My Week with Marilyn*, this was a deliberate move towards edgier, indie-film territory. There would not be so much as a trace of Hermione in *Wallflower*'s Sam.

Alongside all this activity, there were Emma's continuing fashion interests. In December 2010, she announced a link-up with Italian designer Alberta Ferretti to produce a new line of organic and Fair Trade clothing. 'She wrote to me and said, "I saw what you did with People Tree and I think it's a great idea and will you do something with me?"'

The collection featured polka dots, checks and a self-explanatory item called the Emma Blazer. The clothes would have a 'classic, Jane Birkin vibe', Emma said, name-checking the 1960s actress and singer who shot to fame gasping and moaning her way through the 1969 hit record 'Je T'aime . . . Moi Non Plus'.

Emma's approach to her fashion collaborations was a disarmingly simple one: 'I will work for anyone for free if they are prepared to make their clothing Fair Trade organic,' she said.

In January 2011, she unveiled the second instalment of her People Tree collection. The label clearly valued Emma's input and involvement: founder Safia Minney and Misato, one of the label's key designers, flew out to America to work with her on the designs while she was studying at Brown. 'Together, we decided on all the colours, fabrics, shapes and craft skills,' Emma said. 'Most of all, we took care to design a really wearable collection that truly celebrates the traditional skills of People Tree's Fair Trade groups around the world. Fashion is a great way to empower people and give them skills. Rather than give cash to charity, you can help people by buying the clothes they make and supporting things they take pride in. I think young people like me are becoming increasingly aware of the humanitarian issues surrounding fast fashion and want to make good choices, but there aren't many options out there.'

Emma was front and centre in the photographs to illustrate the collection, too, wearing a thigh-high dress and brown boots while posing in a field next to an old motorbike.

There was more lucrative fashion news involving Emma in the spring of 2011: it was claimed she was about to sign a six-figure deal to become the latest ambassador for French makeup firm Lancôme. It's believed the campaign would be shot by Emma's favourite fashion photographer Mario Testino. 'It's so exciting,' she said. 'I can't wait to start shooting. Although I don't wear much makeup, I'm a big fan of Lancôme products, especially their mascara.'

With university, film projects, two fashion collections and a major makeup deal pending, there was only one word for Emma's lifestyle: workaholic. 'I am always working, I am addicted to work,' she said. 'My head needs to rest. I don't have an ordinary day because I'm trapped between two different lives. One day I'm filming, the next I'm off to college, the next day I'm home, then I'm designing clothes. There are no typical days for me.'

But whatever she does – film, fashion or education – there is one thing that Emma will never be able to get away from: all roads will always lead back to Hermione Granger. 'A lot of my getting this part was serendipity,' she admitted to Sky News. 'It happened when I was very young. It was one role and it transformed the whole of my life. But it doesn't necessarily mean that this is what's going to make me happy. I want to be able to explore a few other things.'

On 7 July 2011, 21 year old Emma Watson stood on a purpose-built stage in London's Trafalgar Square wearing a pale blue Oscar de la Renta ball gown. Around her was a sea of fans who'd camped out for days to stake their claims on the best spots for the final Potter premiere. Sections of the crowd were chanting her name. Accompanying Emma on the stage were the main players in the Harry Potter saga, including producer David Heyman, final director David Yates, Daniel Radcliffe, Rupert Grint and J.K. Rowling. Looking out across the sea of faces, Emma Watson was feeling emotional.

Things had not gone entirely smoothly for Emma on the run up to the release of the final film. Headlines in late April had claimed she was quitting her course at Brown University because of bullying. The story that fellow students had quoted lines at her from the Potter films during classes was cited as one of the incidents that had pushed her out. Emma took to the Internet – a sure sign that something had really gotten to her – to set the record straight. 'Dear all,' she wrote in a message posted during the Royal Wedding on 29 April, a move perhaps designed to keep the rebuttal low-key. 'I felt the need to let you all know the reason I took a semester off from Brown had nothing to do with bullying as the media have been suggesting recently. I have never been bullied in my life and certainly never at Brown. This "10 points to Gryffindor" incident never even happened. I feel the need to say this because accusing Brown students of something as serious as bullying and this causing me to leave seems beyond unfair. Please don't try and speculate about what I might do in September – no one can possibly know because I don't even know yet!'

By the time of the final film's release, Emma announced

she had made her decision – she was going to do her third year of university in another country: Britain. 'I haven't left Brown. I'm still enrolled at Brown. I'm going to Oxford in the fall to study English for a year. I'll go back to the States to do my last year. I took a semester off, but my credits actually count as an advance, so I'm no further behind. I'm still technically going into my third year.' Emma Watson was coming home.

Back in Trafalgar Square, the combination of a three thousand-strong crowd and the gushing words of praise from Emma's collaborators proved too much, especially when she tried to thank J.K. Rowling: 'Jo, thank you for writing these amazing books and for being...' with that, the actress began to cry. 'That's it I've gone. You're such a role model to me in real life. Thank you to Rupert for making me laugh, you've been such a great brother. And thank you to Dan – same thing. I will miss you so much.'

The final film was released – this time in 3D – on 15 July, with some cinemas organising special post-midnight screenings for fans keen to be the first to see it. It's a very different beast from the previous Potters. The storytelling shackles that have tied the films down for a decade finally slip away for *Deathly Hallows Part 2*. There are no long explanatory sequences designed to set up plot lines for future films. They aren't needed. All that's required is for dragons to be ridden, wizarding schools to be reduced to rubble and Dark Lords to be vanquished. And, of course, for Hermione and Ron to kiss. Their slamming snog – which puts the rather bloodless peck shared by Harry and Ginny Weasley to shame – is a key moment of relief in the middle of all the death and destruction. According to director David Yates, the success of the scene was down to Emma: 'When we went for the first take,' he told ITV1, 'she [Emma] just made up her mind ... let's do this properly. So she grabbed hold of Rupert and just went for it.' The look on Watson's face when Ron later describes Hermione as his girlfriend for the first time is priceless.

The 3D effects are low-key to the point of being hard to spot, though there's something deeply satisfying about seeing 3D Dementors floating eerily over Hogwarts. The effect truly comes into its own with the piece by piece destruction of Voldemort, as bits of the Dark Lord appear to flutter over the audience's heads. Emma herself was initially unconvinced by the introduction of 3D into the series. She was eventually won round. 'It's done really elegantly and subtly,' she told Radio 1 after seeing the film. 'Things don't jump out at you. It brings you in.'

The twice-filmed epilogue of the grown-up trio is thankfully free of creaky ageing make-up effects – Emma looks largely like you'd expect her to but with a more grown-up haircut. The trio are now adults and a new generation of Weasleys and Potters are heading for Hogwarts. Then ... the credits roll and the most successful film series of all time is over. 'It's epic times four,' was Emma's verdict of the film when asked by the BBC's Edith Bowman. 'It's so dramatic, I was crying like a baby at the end.'

Reviewers, many of whom had fallen in and out of love with the series over the years, were near unanimous that, this time, the film-makers had got it right. *The Guardian* was clear that 'the Potter saga could hardly have ended on a better note than this final movie. With one miraculous flourish of its wand, the franchise has restored the essential magic to the Potter legend, zapping us all with a cracking final chapter. It's dramatically satisfying, spectacular and terrifically exciting.'

'Our central threesome do not disappoint,' said the *Daily Telegraph*. 'Radcliffe's erstwhile plankishness has transformed into a heroic stoicism, Watson has perfected the requisite winsome, fearful look, panting and gasping with the best of them and even Grint can now do "emotional", pulling off a big scene in which one of his brothers is slain. This is monumental cinema, awash with gorgeous tones and carrying an ultimate message that will resonate with every viewer, young or old: there is darkness in all of us, but we can overcome it.'

Time Out: 'Everyone brings their A game here, notably director David Yates and screenwriter Steve Kloves, who balance the source novel's head-spinning blend of action, emotion and narrative intrigue with absolute confidence: one lengthy flashback sequence midway through is arguably the dramatic high point of the entire series and even the sugary sweet coda, so mawkish on the page, becomes a thing of quiet beauty. The special effects are phenomenal, bringing to the magical shenanigans a tactile solidity which has been missing in previous episodes, while Yates's use of 3D is never intrusive, and occasionally breathtaking.'

With the release of the final Potter film, Emma Watson's first professional acting job had finally come to an end – and in her words it was a 'heck of a first job'. It would stay with her forever, not only in terms of the fame it brought her, but also how she would conduct her acting career in the future: 'When I've signed on for other projects, people don't really understand why I get so jumpy and quite concerned,' Emma told ITV1's *Daybreak*. 'I think it's because I signed on for one thing [Harry Potter] and it became a 12-year project. I realise everything else isn't going to be like that but ... I can't believe what it turned into. Jo wrote this incredible female role. I think it's unprecedented because she's not just an equal to the boys, in some respects you can see that she's a stronger fighter. She's a stronger witch – that just doesn't happen in blockbuster movies. Women tend to be these generally pretty sidekicks. And Hermione isn't that at all.'

Emma Watson is an anomaly, a blip in an otherwise crushingly predictable set of show-business rules. The 'journey' for so many young stars – after that initial burst – is expected to be a downward one. Young, beautiful, talented and rich? Off to rehab you go, preferably via a courtroom and an unedifying fall from grace.

It's an offscreen drama that Emma has resolutely refused to be cast in. 'I think it's hard,' she says, when asked about why many of her contemporaries find it so difficult to stay on the rails. 'I can totally understand why they go nuts with the level of interest in their lives and the pressure to be perfect – and they're teenagers. And that's what you do: you screw up. It's really hard, so I would never criticise that.'

The nurturing and protective environment of Leavesden

and the protection of the older Potter actors seems to have been a major factor in Emma and the others exiting the franchise with so few scars. 'There's an awful lot of so-called "child stars" who get sucked into this business, and next thing you know they're 15 and in rehab,' Robbie Coltrane said. 'That hasn't happened here. If anyone came here and said a rude thing about them, I think 300 strong men would leap into action and kill.'

It's telling the number of times the 1960s is referenced with Emma Watson. Harvey Weinstein compares her to model Jean Shrimpton; she references sixties muse Jane Birkin and walks into a hair salon with a picture of Mia Farrow, asking to be made to look like her. In many ways, Emma Watson is a performer out of her time, with more in common with actresses of the 1960s such as Julie Christie, Vanessa Redgrave and the late Susannah York. She's glamorous, well brought up, yet committed and active in social and humanitarian issues.

We expect more of Emma than a Lindsay Lohan and a Miley Cyrus – and we are rarely, if ever, disappointed. It's a measure of how much we have invested in Emma that being seen in the same cab as someone like Razorlight's Johnny Borrell, wearing a short skirt or having a haircut is seen to send out such shockwaves. But maybe, with the responsibility of representing the Potter empire receding, the shackles are starting to come off. 'I wished I'd done more naughty things,' she told the *Sun*. 'I'm ready to start taking risks.'

Emma's background – the word 'privileged' is not too wide of the mark – meant that fame was never going to be her salvation. She would have done perfectly well without it. It's a side issue that is an inconvenience rather than a reason for living. 'I have enough to hold me together without fame,' she points out. This means the way she deals with it is very different from many of her contemporaries. 'That's how I am. Fame never attracted me. Actually, I'm quite shy, I've never liked attention and money. I feel myself a little bit like *Finding Nemo*'s Dory [the fish with a non-existent memory]. I just keep swimming and don't turn around to watch the mess.'

Emma is neither the first nor the last performer to be the product of what used to be called a 'broken home', but her way of dealing with it has been refreshing to say the least. No self-pity or woe-is-me here, just a heads-down, let's-get-on-with-it attitude coupled with an adaptability that treated the Leavesden Studios as a consistent and remarkably nourishing environment. She didn't grow up in Hollywood or even Oxford: she grew up in an old aircraft factory. 'Harry Potter was entirely filmed in a studio in the middle of nowhere, in the most stinky, leaky, falling-apart shed you can ever imagine, and I went to that place every day for ten years. Yes, I made these extremely famous movies, but everything was inside a bubble, with the same people. Everything was really contained. The crew became my family. I wasn't involved with all the Hollywood stuff, that would've made me feel really disturbed and lost. No one ever treated me as if I was different from anyone, nobody treated us as stars.'

Emma has even dared to use a word you very rarely hear these days in an effort to explain why she has thrived under such unusual conditions. 'There's also my *breeding*. My family – and I can't really make enough emphasis in this – isn't interested in the artistic environment at all. In my house, nobody watches movies, they are academic-oriented, they are just not interested in this. My being an actress is not their dream made true. They just want to watch me happy. Their main focus is not my stardom.'

She may have been born in France and lived in Oxford and London, but Emma Watson spent most of her time on the set of the Harry Potter films, either racing around on her bike in the less-than-salubrious environment of Leavesden Studios in Watford or out on location in far-flung corners of Britain. 'I don't think I'm as black and white as the media like to make me out. I'm not your classic public-school girl because I've been brought up here, in Watford. And I've met and worked with people from a million different backgrounds. Everyone's going to think different things about me and I can't control that. You can't please everyone. And that's something that I'm learning.'

It has sometimes been said that working on the film series is referred to as the 'Potter Pension', thanks to the long-term and financially rewarding nature of the task. But for Emma the investment has been an emotional one – the men and women who worked on the films became her family and have given her a consistency that was lacking in her life split between her parents. 'God knows how many hours – years – I've spent on set,' she told *The Times*. 'But my driver Nigel was trying to work out how many hours he'd driven in the car, and he says the distance was twice around the world.'

The questions about Emma's childhood would have a

remarkably similar ring to them over the years: Are you sad that you missed out on your childhood by being involved in the Potter films from such a young age? 'It's difficult to talk about the things we missed when we gained so much,' she pointed out. 'We probably had to grow up a lot quicker than normal children, we had a lot of responsibility. In that sense, it was difficult and a lot of pressure, but the experience has been so amazing and unique.'

It's an unprecedented achievement for an ensemble cast – particularly such a young one – to emerge intact from such a marathon bout of filmmaking. To have the same people playing the same roles from such a young age until adulthood is unique. It will be a very long time until it's equalled – if ever. 'I think it's amazing to look back and think I've been part of eight big, big, big films. I'm so proud,' Emma said. 'It feels like a real accomplishment. I actually find the earlier ones a lot easier to watch, because I'm able to detach myself from my *young* self a lot more. Whereas maybe watching the fifth or the fourth one, I'm just a couple of years younger – it's *me*, a younger me. I find that more cringey. It feels like I'm watching someone different on screen when I'm nine or ten.'

Emma's relationship with the co-stars who have shared those eight big films is the one that's fascinated the public the most – a public who saw no reason why the fairytale couldn't have a logical conclusion. As we saw earlier, Daniel Radcliffe has said that there was never anybody he really fancied in the cast, in spite of the constant expectation from fans that he and Emma were dating. The fans always seemed to expect that the young Potter stars spent all their spare hours having sleepovers and larking about together. They have all toed the party line on this, politely pointing out that, as they spend such a vast amount of time on set together, it would be reasonable to spend spare moments with family and friends back home. Emma admits that hanging out together off set would be 'overload'. 'I love them, but I need to see other friends off set. They're like my siblings now.'

Only Tom Felton (Draco Malfoy) seems to have broken ranks with a rather frosty response to one journalist who asked whether he had seen Emma now that Potter filming was finished. 'I haven't seen so much of her,' he told the *Daily Mail*. 'She is very professional and seems like an intelligent lady.'

But it's the onscreen relationships between the young stars that set the Potter series apart from other film franchises. As cinemagoers, we knew where we stood with the world of Harry Potter. James Bond changes – Pierce Brosnan one minute, Daniel Craig the next – but the Potter kids remained the same. 'The audience and fans have a relationship [with the actors] that goes back ten years, and that's something really magical,' director David Yates told the *Daily Telegraph*. 'That is actually more important than all the battles, frankly, and all the special effects, and everything, because they are going through the cycle of life that we've all been through.'

It's the young actors who are the secret ingredient to the Potter franchise and its multi-billion-pound success. It certainly isn't critical acclaim that's led people to pay their money at the box office for the best part of a decade. Harry

Potter films rarely get the plaudits bestowed on less successful films. Their performers don't appear onstage at the Oscars when Best Actor or Best Actress statuettes are being handed out and the films don't top the critics' lists of their favourites. As *Sunday Times* film critic Cosmo Landesman pointed out, 'If the Harry Potters really are such great films, why is it that they are never cited in reputable newspaper and film magazine polls of top films? In both *The Times* 100 Best Films of the Decade and the *Sunday Times* Top 40 Films of the Millennium – devised by polling teams of critics for their opinion – none of the Harry Potter films makes an appearance. Is this just filmic snobbery? It seems not. The same is true of best-film lists found in film magazines such as *Empire* and *Total Film*, even when the polls are based on readers' votes.'

As it happens, Emma was given an award for Child Performance of the Year by none other than *Total Film* in 2004, and *Empire* magazine gave the Potter films an Outstanding Contribution Award in 2006. But Emma's awards have tended to be of a more populist nature: National Film Award for Best Female Performer and Nickelodeon Kids' Choice Award for Best Movie Actress.

Any lingering feeling that the Harry Potter films hadn't quite received their due was finally dispelled in February 2011, when it was announced that the franchise would be honoured with an award for Outstanding British Contribution to Cinema at the British Academy of Film and Television Arts (BAFTA) awards. Despite a decade of astonishing success, getting the nod from BAFTA seemed to mean a great deal to Emma: 'This is a huge honour! I am so proud to have been part of the incredible team both in front and behind the camera that made these films. Thank you to Jo Rowling for writing such wonderful books, to David Heyman for shepherding us all through the past ten years and to all the loyal fans who have been with us throughout.'

Producer David Heyman admitted he was baffled as to why BAFTA had so far not found a space for Harry Potter in its heart: 'It's really wonderful that it's the whole franchise being recognised and it's a collective award. Each film has anywhere between 2,000 and 6,000 people working on it and so really the award is for each and every one of us. We are like a family.'

Emma made quite a splash that BAFTA weekend in February 2011. She attended several pre-awards parties in the run-up to the ceremony, including one at the Almada Bar in Mayfair to celebrate the success of Colin Firth and *The King's Speech*. But it was Emma who made the morning papers, dressed in a £1,700 leather Burberry coat and sporting a slightly longer version of her famed pixie cut. She then went to the nearby Mahiki nightclub, arriving in the back of film mogul Harvey Weinstein's Rolls-Royce. When she left at 3am, Emma was in danger of being mobbed by autograph hunters and photographers. Harvey Weinstein – clearly looking to protect one of his prize assets – took hold of Emma and guided her safely through the crowd.

The following night she was at another pre-awards party, this time at Mark's Club, again in Mayfair. The normally cautious Emma was caught out by photographers as she arrived at this private members' club – pictures of her showing more flesh than she'd intended appeared in the following day's papers: WHAT SHE WOULDN'T GIVE FOR A CLOAK OF INVISIBILITY RIGHT NOW! EMMA WATSON FLASHES AFTER 'WARDROBE MALFUNCTION', crowed one headline the next morning.

On Sunday, 13 February, Emma arrived at the BAFTAs ceremony itself at the Royal Opera House in Covent Garden. She was there to present the award for Outstanding British Film to the makers of *The King's Speech* (which would go on, at the end of February, to win four Oscars: Best Film, Best Original Screenplay, Best Actor for Firth and Best Director for Tom Hooper; *Deathly Hallows Part 1* was nominated for Best Art Direction and Best Visual Effects, but would not win an Oscar). Emma was also part of the Potter party to receive a BAFTA for the franchise's contribution to the industry. On the red carpet, she stood with J. K. Rowling, who described Emma as being 'like my daughter'.

Emma was wearing a floor-length, flesh-coloured Valentino dress and, as ever, she caught the eye of the fashion writers. 'Harry Potter star Emma Watson led the charge last night for home-grown beauty as she shone on the red carpet at the Royal Opera House in a stunning floor-length nude gown by Valentino,' said the *Daily Mail*. 'She was hoping not to repeat her wardrobe malfunction of a pre-BAFTAs party on Saturday night in London, when she inadvertently flashed her chest [when] some tape keeping her plunging frock in place gave way.'

Emma took to the stage along with Rupert Grint, Jo

Rowling, three of the Potter directors, and producers David Baron and David Heyman. 'Over 6,000 people worked on each of the films,' Heyman said. 'I'd like to say a huge thank you to BAFTA for this honour. Over the past decade, we've had the privilege of working with some of the finest people, in an atmosphere filled with pride but with no ego, working on glorious fiction created by Jo Rowling. We became a family of sorts. We had an awful lot of fun – our amazing cast, Dan, Rupert, Emma and a host of others and our incomparable crew. I'd like to thank Jo Rowling for encouraging parents and children to share the pleasure of reading.'

J. K. Rowling added, 'It's very strange to look back over seven films and remember how wary I was of letting anyone put Harry on the big screen. I kept saying no. It was David Heyman who persuaded me. He's been there from start to finish. I need to say publicly how right I was to trust him, how much I owe him and how grateful I am to him. Being involved in these films has been one of the best experiences of my life.'

But it's never been about awards. The thing that has brought cinemagoers back time and time again was the opportunity of seeing performers – and their characters – grow before their very eyes. With that opportunity has come a great deal of fame, money, responsibility and pressure. 'There have been times when I've wanted to throw my hands up and go, "Take it all away, give it to someone else; it's too much, I can't cope; I can't deal with it, I don't want it," because it has been pretty overwhelming,' Emma said. 'But, now it's coming to an end, I can step back and really start to appreciate it. Now it feels good – it feels so satisfying – to have completed all seven of the books, all eight of the movies, and seen Hermione through from beginning to end. I can't believe I've actually managed it. What Dan, Rupert and I have done is unique. To inhabit these characters for ten years, through a period of our lives when we've changed so much, feels like such an achievement.'

Daniel Radcliffe quipped, 'Being in Harry Potter is a lot like being in the Mafia, in that, once you're in, you're never really out. We are inextricably linked to each other for the rest of our lives.'

Emma seems very aware that, for all the pleasure there is to be found in being so famous for her role as Hermione Granger, there is – and will always be – a downside: 'The best thing about being involved in Harry Potter is that you can make a six-year-old girl or boy's day by giving them a handshake, and it's so easy. It costs me so little to make someone incredibly happy, so that's amazing and I've walked away and thought, God, I'm so lucky to be in a position that people are that excited to meet me. It's amazing. The downside is that the level of curiosity into your life means that it becomes quite intrusive and the level of criticism is hard to deal with sometimes. It can make you really insecure.'

Now the Potter achievement is complete, it leaves Emma Watson with the very straightforward problem of what to do next. By her own admission, she never needs to work another day in her life if she chooses not to. 'I'm going to say something really sad. Knowing that there's still more to come from me, it feels very strange to feel like you're retiring when you're 20 years old. But it does feel that way. I've spent ten years making these movies and I just hope that the second part of my life is as incredible as the first half.'

But perhaps things were getting a little *too* incredible; Emma maintained an astonishing pace during February and March 2011, jetting into London while trying to maintain her studies back in America. As well as attending the BAFTAs and the inevitable round of parties, she attended the *Elle* Style Awards wearing a nude-coloured Hakaan mini dress with daring cutaway sides.

Emma was there to be named as the magazine's Style Icon and received her award from British design legend Vivienne Westwood, who admitted to the celeb-packed crowd that she had no idea who the actress was. 'I was supposed to welcome and to announce the winner of the Style Icon – which I'm going to do – and I was given this text about this woman and how amazing she is,' she said. 'Yesterday I was asked, "This lady would like you to present it to her if she wins." But I didn't know who she was. They said Emma Watson. I said, "Who is Emma Watson?" I never watch television, I don't read fashion magazines. They said she used to be in Harry Potter, and I said, "I've never seen Harry Potter." They said he has this girl friend called Hermione and I said, "Oh, she's lovely." So I must have absorbed something of her. So I would like to give this award to Emma who I've just met.'

Elle editor Lorraine Candy certainly knew all about

Emma Watson. 'She's got a very distinct individual look,' Candy said. 'We always say at *Elle*, "It's not what you wear, it's the way you wear it," and she's got such spirit, Emma. I think that makes her stylish.'

Emma was also putting the finishing touches to *My Week with Marilyn* while preparing for *The Perks of Being a Wallflower*, as well as fulfilling her other fashion commitments. Then there were preparations for the final Potter premiere to think about. It was announced that the unveiling of *Harry Potter and the Deathly Hallows Part 2* would be the first red-carpet film event to take place in London's Trafalgar Square, as it had been decided that Leicester Square, where the previous premieres have been held, would be just too small for the opening of the last Potter movie. The promotional duties would be harder than ever and would take her around the world.

Something had to give. On 7 March 2011, something did. Emma posted a message on her website: 'Hi everyone – As you know, I love Brown and I love studying pretty much more than anything but recently I've had so much to juggle that being a student AND fulfilling my other commitments has become a little impossible. I've decided to take a bit of time off to completely finish my work on Harry Potter (the last one comes out this summer) and to focus on my other professional and acting projects. I will still be working towards my degree . . . it's just going to take me a semester or two longer than I thought :) Hope you are all well! Thank you for all your continuing support.'

Emma was under more scrutiny than ever – even she couldn't juggle so many different projects and maintain her education, especially given the fact that her university was halfway around the world. Her spokesman refused to confirm how quickly she was withdrawing from Brown, but, given the amount of work that lay ahead of her, the strong suggestion was that she was ending her studies immediately.

There have been so few breaks in Emma Watson's life so far, it's not surprising that she finally had to take her foot off the pedal. Despite all the projects, she still appears to be in something of a holding pattern, waiting for the next really big challenge to present itself. 'I want to figure out how I feel about everything first,' she told *Elle*. 'Maybe I'll keep acting, maybe I won't. I just want to find something where I feel I *have* to do this. Maybe that'll happen when I read a script. It felt like that with Hermione. I want to feel like that again.'

When that feeling comes it will be accompanied by an inevitable increase in publicity, scrutiny and pressure, though, if anyone has the tools to cope with it, it's Emma Watson: 'To be honest, I was thrown into the mosh pit known as the red carpet at 11 years old. I'm just used to it all. I know what to expect. I've seen it all.'

The scrutiny centres on her acting, her hair, her clothes and her lifestyle. And her love life. Every look and gesture carried out in public – or sometimes in private – has been captured, discussed and commented on across the world. Not the easiest environment to build a relationship in. 'I'm very romantic and of course I want to be in love,' she told the *Sun*. 'I've been in love once in my life, but it was complicated. I can't tell you who it was because it wouldn't be fair to any others. But I can say I've never had my heart broken. I like men with quick wit, good conversation and a great sense of humour. I love banter. I want a man to like me for me – I want him to be authentic. But men don't really ask me out. And I don't get marriage proposals any more, either. It's not happening there!'

Apart from Emma's father Chris, there is one man who has been consistent throughout this story – and that's Potter producer David Heyman. He has a Harry Potter poster on the wall of his office – it's signed by all three of the young stars: 'You're a WICKED producer!' says the message from Rupert Grint. 'Thank goodness I went to the theatre. Love, Dan' is Radcliffe's contribution. Emma's? Well, it couldn't be more Watsonesque: 'To David, thank you is not a strong enough word for my gratitude'. Inevitably, the handwriting is impeccable.

It's Heyman whom Emma credits with keeping her and the other young stars sane through what was essentially an insane process. 'Emma is astonishingly bright and just anxious to move forward with life,' Heyman told the *Los Angeles Times*. 'She's been amazing to watch. She has these choices. She could be an actress or a model, but with her studies and success she could also be a lawyer. She could also be an artist . . . It's pretty amazing to see.'

Emma Watson, it appears, can do anything. 'I want to work in every single genre,' she said. 'If anyone will say anything about my career, [I want it to be that] I was able to do lots of different things and I didn't just play one person in lots of different films, and my role choices were diverse and interesting. I'd love to do a period drama, a musical, a crazy Baz Lurhmann *Moulin Rouge* . . . I'd love to do a small independent film. I'd love to do a French film. I want to do everything.'

There's no reason to doubt her. Emma Watson has shown time and again that she can 'step up'. She's done it before – it's certain she will do it again. 'For me, this is just the beginning. I've only shown a little bit of what I can do. There is so much more to come.'